Design in the 20th Century

Form Follows Function?

Susan Lambert

Victoria & Albert Museum

Acknowledgements

This book is one of a series to grow out of and complement the 20th Century Gallery at the Victoria and Albert Museum which opened in October 1992. It owes much to conversations with the Gallery's project team: Jeremy Aynsley, Kevin Edge, Clare Graham, Brian Griggs and Margaret Knight. I would like to thank them and everyone else who contributed advice and information much of which has been recycled here, especially Craig Clunas, Neil Harvey, Amy de la Haye, Gwyn Miles, John Murdoch, Jennifer Opie, Charles Saumarez Smith, Michael Snodin, John Styles, Eric Turner, Clive Wainwright, Christopher Wilk and Gareth Williams. I would also like to thank everyone in the Prints, Drawings and Paintings Collection for their help and understanding, and especially Stephen Astley for lending me his library.

The text draws considerably on the literature quoted in the Further Reading. I would like to thank all the authors for the inspiration and guidance their work has provided, and Gillian Naylor in addition for help with sources and Penny Sparke for reading and commenting on the text at a time when she was extremely busy. With a quotation as a starting point, I felt it especially appropriate to use the words of those who supported and reacted to it. Without Tim and Charlotte Benton and Dennis Sharp's invaluable *Form and function a source book of the history of architecture and design 1890-1939*, which makes so many foreign texts easily accessible in English, this would not have been possible. The reproductions except where stated otherwise appear courtesy of the Board of Trustees of the Victoria and Albert Museum. I would like to thank everyone who organised and took the photographs including Philip Barnard, Clare Browne, Brenda Norrish, Danny McGrath, Clare Phillips, Eoin Shalloo, Christine Smith and Philip Spruyt de Bay. Very special thanks go to Moira Thunder who co-ordinated this work so efficiently.

I would also like to thank John Taylor for his sympathetic editing, Karen Wilks for her imaginative approach to the design, and Jennifer Blain and Lesley Burton for seeing the text through the press with so much patience and flexibility.

First published by the Victoria & Albert Museum 1993
© The Trustees of the Victoria & Albert Museum
All rights reserved. No part of this publication may be reproduced, stored in a retrieval system, or transmitted, in any form or by any means, electronic, mechanical, photocopying, recording or otherwise without the prior written permission of the Trustees of the Victoria & Albert Museum

British Library Cataloguing-in-Publication Data
A catalogue record for this book is available from the British Library

ISBN 1 85177 122 0

Designed by Karen Wilks

Printed in England by BAS Printers

Contents

1. Guaranty Building, Buffalo, New York, a steel-framed building, designed by Louis Sullivan (USA, 1856-1924), 1895. Henry Fuermann & Sons, Chicago

This thirteen-story building, completed at about the time that Sullivan was writing 'The tall office building artistically considered', must have been in his mind as he considered the relationship between form and function. Its design expresses his belief that the outward form of the building should reflect its inner uses. The office floors, having the same function, are undifferentiated in their external detail.

Strength, Utility and Grace: the Vitruvian Triad

The maxim 'form follows function' is credited to the American architect, Louis Sullivan (1856-1924), and certainly it plays a central role in his architectural doctrine. Words similar to these have been interpreted in different ways at different moments in history. This chapter sets the debate which has surrounded them during this century in a wider context.

Sullivan's theories on the relationship of form and function were first published in 1896 in an article entitled 'The tall office building artistically considered'[1] in *Lippincott's*, a Philadelphian review encompassing literature, science and education (Fig. 1). Here he presented the tall office building as a new, 'vital problem, pressing for a true solution' which he claimed was contained within its elements. These he described as '1st, a story below-ground, containing boiler, engines of various sorts…2nd, a ground floor …devoted to stores, banks, or other establishments requiring large area, ample spacing, ample light, and great freedom of access. 3rd, a second story readily accessible by stairways – this space usually in large subdivisions, with corresponding liberality in structural spacing and expanse of glass and breadth of external openings. 4th, above this an indefinite number of stories of offices piled tier upon tier, one tier just like another tier, one office just like all the other offices – an office being similar to a cell in a honeycomb, merely a compartment, nothing more. 5th, and last, at the top of this pile is placed a space or story that, as related to the life and usefulness of the structure, is purely physiological in its nature – namely, the attic…The space is filled with tanks… and mechanical etcetera that supplement and complement the force-originating plant hidden below-ground in the cellar. Finally, or at the beginning rather, there must be on the ground floor a main aperture or entrance common to all occupants or patrons of the building.'[2]

He then went on to explain that 'In turn, these purely arbitary units of structure form…the true basis of the artistic development of the exterior…Beginning with the first story, we give this main entrance that attracts the eye to its location, and the remainder of the story we treat in a more or less liberal, expansive, sumptuous way – a way based exactly on the practical necessities, but expressed with a sentiment of largeness and freedom. The second story we treat in a similar way, but usually with milder pretension. Above this, throughout the indefinite number of typical office tiers, we take our cue from the individual cell…and we, without more ado, make them look all alike because they are all alike. This brings us to the attic, which, having no division into office-cells, and no special requirement for lighting, gives us the power to show by means of its broad expanse of wall, and its dominating weight and character, that which is the fact – namely, that the series of office tiers has come definitely to an end.'[3]

He justified his solution by an analogy with nature: 'All things in nature have…a form, an outward semblance, that tells us what they are, that distinguishes them from ourselves and from each other. Unfailingly in nature these shapes express the inner life, the native quality, of the animal, tree, bird, fish…It seems ever as though the

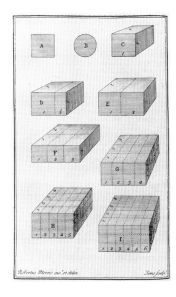

life and the form were absolutely one and inseparable...Whether it be the sweeping eagle in his flight or the open apple-blossom, the toiling work-horse, the blithe swan, the branching oak, the winding stream at its base, the drifting clouds, over all the coursing sun, form ever follows function, and this is the law.'[4]

It is, he said, a law that art should not violate. An architect 'must cause a building to grow naturally, logically and poetically out of its conditions' for 'the true work of the architect is to organize, integrate and glorify UTILITY'.[5]

It is the 'law' itself 'form ever follows function', refined in his later writings to the alliterated maxim 'form follows function', for which Sullivan is responsible. The ideas contained within his teachings, however, have a long history stretching as far back as the writings of Vitruvius (active 46–30 BC), a Roman architect of no special significance were he not the author of the only architectural treatise to have survived from antiquity. In this, architecture is presented as a science which can be comprehended rationally, with 'strength', 'utility' and 'grace' as its essential elements. Republished repeatedly from the Renaissance with different emphases, it has continued to contribute to the theory of design even within the twentieth century. For example, a strikingly functionalist interpretation by the French engineer, archaeologist and architectural historian, François-Auguste Choisy (1841–1904), was issued in 1909[6] and a version of the triad 'commodity, firmness and delight' provided the structuring principle for an exhibition held in London in 1938 of the MARS (Modern Architectural Research) Group,[7] which advocated the introduction of a Rationalist approach to architecture in Britain.

Belief in the fundamental rationality of the beautiful was characteristic of much Western thought throughout the Renaissance and Enlightenment. The principles of unity, proportion and suitability were set forth by Leon Battista Alberti (1404–1472), the archetypal universal man, in his *De re aedificatoria*, the first architectural treatise of the Renaissance, issued in 1452. His thoughts on suitability, read with twentieth-century hindsight, take on a functionalist aspect:

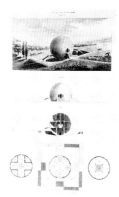

4. 'Shelter for the Rural Guards.' Illustration to Claude-Nicolas Ledoux, *L'architecture considerée sous le rapport de l'art*, Paris 1804, p.316.

Geometric forms became increasingly conspicuous in architectural design in France towards 1800. Ledoux designed cubic, pyramidal and cylindrical buildings as well as several spherical ones.

5. Frontispiece to Marc-Antoine Laugier, *Essai sur l'architecture*, Paris 1755.

The frontispiece illustrates the primitive hut which Laugier argued was the basic model of all architecture. Le Corbusier knew Laugier's writings and his aesthetic was derived from similar principles. Laugier's writings were as fundamental to Neo-classicism as Le Corbusier's to Modernism.

'To every member…ought to be allotted its fit Place and proper Situation; not less than Dignity requires, not greater than Conveniency demands; not in an impertinent or indecent place, but in a Situation so proper itself, that it could be set nowhere else more fitly. Nor should the part of the Structure, that is to be of the greatest Honour be thrown into a remote Corner…nor that which should be most private, be set in too conspicuous a place'.[8]

Similar ideas run through much Classicist doctrine. Robert Morris (1701-1754), the theoretician of English Palladianism, recommended ancient models because he saw in them 'those unerring Rules, those perfect Standards of the Law of Reason and Nature, founded upon Beauty and Necessity'[9]. Thomas Sheraton (1751-1806), cabinet-maker and draughtsman, captioned the frontispiece to his *Cabinet-maker and upholsterer's drawing book* 'Time alters fashions and frequently obliterates the works of art and ingenuity; but that which is founded on Geometry and real science, will remain unalterable'[10]. Claude-Nicolas Ledoux (1736-1806), an extreme exponent of French Neo-classicism, claimed after describing an ornamented barn that all 'is motivated by necessity'[11]. All three stressed the importance in design of simple geometric shapes of the kind favoured by the Modernists although there is no suggestion that the shapes emerged from their function independent of aesthetic intention or emotive impact (Figs. 2-4).

The economic simplicity associated with twentieth-century notions of functionalism also has earlier origins. Marc-Antoine Laugier (1713-1769), a French priest who encapsulated the spirit of Neo-classicism in his *Essai sur l'architecture* of 1753, gave protection from the elements as the function underlying the building of houses. Describing the simple means with which primitive man constructed shelter, he claimed 'All the splendours of architecture ever conceived have been modeled on the little rustic hut'[12] (Fig. 5).

Even the word 'function' appears to have played a significant part in the teachings of the Venetian Franciscan, Carlo Lodoli (1690-1761). But although he taught that 'in architecture only that shall show that has a definite function, and which derives from strictest

6-7. Two designs highlighting the symbolic value of form:

6. Plate 6 to Charles Percier and P.F.L. Fontaine, *Recueil de décorations Intérieurs...*, Paris 1801.

According to its designers the form of this 'chair' was based on 'general rules of truth, simplicity and beauty'. Their writings suggest that they subscribed to a functionalist aesthetic. The function of their 'Empire' furniture was, however, to project the power of the Emperor, of whom they were the favoured architects.

necessity',[13] that 'the outside should be indicative of the interior disposition'[14] and that furniture should be fitted to the form of the human body,[15] he was a theoretician, and not a designer, and, like Laugier, did not give three-dimensional form to his theories.

The French architects Charles Percier (1764–1838) and P.F.L. Fontaine (1762–1853) came close to enunciating Sullivan's theory and as creators of the Empire style were prolific in their influence on actual manufactures. In *Recueil de décorations intérieurs...*of 1801 the chair's role is analysed in terms of its interaction with its user: 'Among all the forms of a chair, there are some which are dictated by the shape of our body, by demands of necessity or of comfort …What is there that art could add? It should purify the forms dictated by convenience and combine them with the simplest outlines giving rise from those natural conditions to ornamental motifs which could be adapted to the basic form without ever disguising nature'[16] (Fig. 6).

Functionalism has also played a significant part in appreciation of

Par Percier et Fontaine.

Fauteuil et Vases siécutés à Paris dans la Maison du C. D.....

the Gothic style. By the eighteenth century concentration on its structural raison-d'être had become standard practice in the teaching of architecture in France[17] and its revival in Britain in the nineteenth century was justified partly on functionalist grounds. In 1841, A.W.N.Pugin (1812-1852), the British architect and decorator responsible for the Gothic detailing of the Houses of Parliament, asserted in *The true principles of pointed or christian architecture*: 'The two great rules for design are these: *1st, that there should be no features about a building which are not necessary for convenience, construction, or propriety; 2nd, that all ornament should consist of enrichment of the essential construction of the building*…In pure architecture the smallest detail should *have a meaning or a sense of purpose*.'[18] He drove his view home by speaking disparagingly of the flying buttresses, such an expressive member of Gothic architecture, on Sir Christopher Wren's (1632-1723) Classical St Paul's Cathedral: '*as this style of architecture does not admit of the great principle of decorating utility*, the buttresses, instead of being made *ornamental, are concealed by an enormous screen*, going entirely round *the building. So that in fact one half of the edifice is built to conceal the other*.'[19]

The doctrine of the French architect and restorer, Eugène-Emanuel Viollet-Le-Duc (1814-1879), was especially significant for the twentieth century for his admiration of the Gothic sprang from a search for a contemporary rather than revivalist style. He was drawn to it not through a romantic attachment to what it symbolised but rather on the grounds of its logic: 'Those who pretend to see in Gothic architecture…anything else than the emancipation of a nation of artists and artisans, who, having been taught to reason, reason better than their masters, and with the forces put into their hands, carry them in spite of themselves very far from the goal that at first they wished to reach; those who believed that Gothic architecture is an exception, a caprice of the human mind, have certainly not studied its principle, which is but rigorous application of the system inaugurated by the Romanesque constructors.'[20] Some of his writings also had an overtly functionalist bent: 'If the architects of the twelfth and thirteenth centuries made naves high…it was not with any puerile symbolic intent, rather to

7. 'George Washington' by Horatio Greenough (USA 1805-1852), 1832-41. Marble. Height: 345.5cm. The National Collection, Smithsonian Institution, Washington, D.C.

Greenough was an advocate of the importance of function in design. Here he portrayed George Washington (1732-1799), statesman, general and first president of the United States, in the pose and attire of a Roman emperor. The associative value of imagery has a function.

provide air and light for those great elevated vessels in a gloomy and damp climate; in this, as in all things, they simply followed their reasons'.[21] According to Viollet-Le-Duc the rational approach which created the Gothic would, if applied to contemporary problems, create a style appropriate to the present.[22]

Even the claim that the fulfilment of function was a recipe for beautiful form, seldom made by the Modernists but with which they are associated, had its origins in earlier centuries. It is implied by the French encyclopaedist and man of letters, Denis Diderot (1713-1784), in his statement that 'the beautiful man is he that nature has made to fulfil most easily the two great functions: self preservation and propagation'.[23] A post-Darwinian interpretation even suggests sympathy with the theories of natural selection which underpin another maxim of twentieth-century design: 'fitness for purpose'.[24]

By the nineteenth century such ideas had become part of established aesthetic theory, widely accessible through texts like Archibald Alison's *Essays on the nature and principles of taste*, first published in 1790 and achieving five editions by 1817. Here, building on Edmund Burke's theories on the Sublime,[25] mediated by the Picturesque, it was stated that 'in the Forms of Furniture, of Machines, and of Instruments in the different Arts' a greater part of their beauty arises from 'fitness, or the proper adaptation of Means to an End'; moreover, 'utility' is quoted as one of three important sources of beauty. The argument is supported with specific examples not unlike Le Corbusier's in *Vers une architecture*[26] including a surgeon's knife, the 'wedge-like snout of the Swine, the little sunken eyes, and the whole head, so well adapted to its offices of digging and rooting', a direct quote from Burke with its meaning reversed, and a ship.[27]

Sullivan is, however, more likely to have devised his theories in the light of those of his fellow American, the sculptor Horatio Greenough (1805-1852) (Fig. 7), whose means of addressing his countrymen through rousing articles in periodicals was similar to that of his own. Greenough defined beauty as the promise of function and argued that instead of forcing the functions of every sort of building into one general form, adopting an outward shape for the sake of the eye or of association, without reference to the inner distribution, let us begin from the heart and nucleus and work outward. Embellishment he considered 'false beauty' maintaining that 'the first downward step was *the introduction of the first inorganic, non functional element, whether shape or color'*. The justification for his theories lay like Sullivan's in his belief that such a system reflected the way of nature – that it was God's way.[28]

Theories are readily convertible to the needs of their users. For example the furniture made by Percier and Fontaine, the buildings of Pugin, and the sculptures shaped by Greenough do not, according to a Modernist interpretation of functionalism, reflect their makers' doctrine. The forms of Percier and Fontaine are encrusted with embellishment of an associative and symbolic value which it could be argued would hamper their use as utilitarian accompaniments to ordinary life; Pugin was primarily concerned with the structures of buildings not their plans; and Greenough's sculptures are remarkable only for their respectful furtherance of the Classical tradition.

What differentiates Sullivan's contribution from that of all his predecessors is his application of his law to what became known as the skyscraper, a form of architecture especially associated with the twentieth century, in a manner which, in spite of his free use of ornament, bears some relation to Modernist readings of its meaning. The article on *The tall office building…*makes it clear that he is seeking not an individual or special solution, but for 'a true normal type'.[29] The search for ultimate object types, a logical corollary of the maxim 'form follows function', was to play a significant part in Modernist theory. But, 'forward-looking' as certain aspects of Sullivan's buildings may have been, his greatest significance for the twentieth century lies in the way his aphorism 'form follows function' was taken up and reinterpreted, becoming a constant refrain in twentieth-century design theory.

8. Vase designed by
Kolomon Moser (Austrian,
1868-1918) and made by
the Wiener Werkstätte,
Vienna, Austria, about 1904.
Silver. Height: 20cm.
M.17 – 1982

The Wiener Werkstätte
artists worked with a
range of different metals
cut by machine outside
their workshops. This
reduced the costs of even
luxury products such as
this, gave products from
the workshops by different
designers a shared 'look',
and expressed through
the decorative effect
a commitment to
the machine.

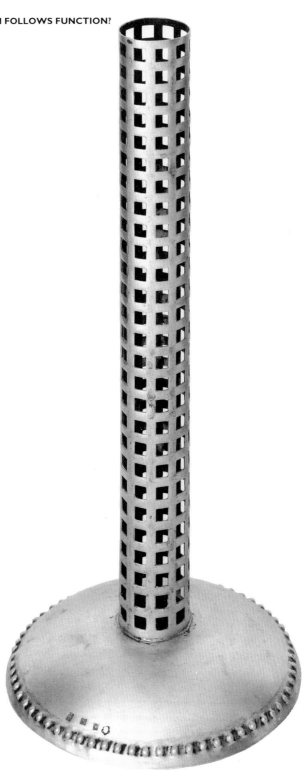

Efficiency Style

If the significance of function in defining form is central to traditional architectural and design theory, why has the term 'functionalism' become almost synonymous with the architecture and design of the Modern Movement, the style which has dominated production in the western world for most of the twentieth century? Is it simply the absence of traditional ornament, or the extent to which notions of function have featured in debate, or is there something distinctive about the Modern Movement's interpretation of function's role?

A large proportion of nineteenth-century design theory was based on a sense that design had gone wrong and that the increased use of powered machines, a developing force since the early eighteenth century, was to blame. The architect, C.R.Cockerell (1788-1863), giving evidence in 1836 to a British Parliamentary Committee on Arts and Manufactures was in tune with much subsequent debate. His statement 'I believe that the attempt to supersede the work of the mind and hand by mechanical process for the sake of economy will always have the effect of degrading and ultimately ruining art'[30] is only one step removed from that of Walter Gropius (1883-1969), architect and Director of the Bauhaus, in the official record of the theory and organisation of the Weimar Bauhaus published in 1923: 'So long…as machine-economy remains an end in itself rather than a means of freeing the intellect from the burden of mechanical labour, the individual will remain enslaved and society disordered'.[31]

Not only was it claimed that machines had usurped the craftsman's position but also that the division of labour encouraged by their management had tended increasingly to separate making from responsibility for the appearance of the product. In addition the speed with which machines work facilitated the manufacture of ever greater numbers of products and, because machines can execute certain tasks only, influenced design in a direction compatible with machine production.[32] This not only affected the form of products but had also, since the introduction of machines in the

9. Dish and cover designed by Henry van de Velde (Belgian, 1863-1957), 1903-4; made by Meissen, Germany, about 1905-12. Porcelain with overglaze enamel colours and gilding. Diameter: 26.2 cm. C.37 – 1990

Meissen commissioned van de Velde after its designs had been criticised as unadventurous at the Paris Exhibition 1900. Van de Velde's decoration consisted only of the gilded linear pattern. Admired by the critics but a poor seller, the traditional flower sprigs were added by Meissen in an attempt to convert it into a commercial success. The piece raises questions about the function of ornament and introduces the practicalities of commerce to the theoretical debate.

10. Bathroom from Shanks & Co., Barrhead. Illustration to Hermann Muthesius, *Das englische Haus*, Berlin 1905, p.237.

Likening the modern bathroom to 'a piece of scientific apparatus', Muthesius claimed that 'If ornament accessories, which always destroy the general appearance of a bathroom, are really kept out, a truly modern character will be achieved'.

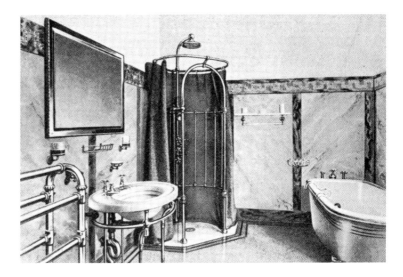

wood-working trades during the nineteenth century, encouraged certain sorts of ornamentation at the expense of others. This proliferation of 'mechanical' ornament was arguably one reason for the reaction against the whole tradition of organic ornament in the years around 1900.

By the turn of the century there was a widespread sense that something had to be done and that the worst excesses of the past could be avoided if a rational 'no nonsense' approach to form, which gave priority to a product's ultimate function in terms of its practical utility, was adopted. Henri van de Velde (1863-1957), the prolific Belgian designer associated with the whiplash motif of Art Nouveau, advised 'never creating anything which has no valid reason for existing',[33] and argued in 1901 that 'any consideration other than utility and function can be dangerous and soon lead to a failure'. Citing locomotives, steamers, machines, bridges, English perambulators, bathroom fittings, and electric hanging-lamps, he claimed them to be beautiful 'because they are exactly what they should be' and remain so 'until greedy mischief-making manufacturers choose to embellish them in their own way and then, utterly disregarding their original necessity, rob them of their forms'[34] (Fig. 9). 'Function' was the guiding principle and 'utility' the first condition of the Wiener Werkstätte (Vienna Workshops 1903-1930), which favoured

11. End piece to
Richard Riemerschmid,
'Der Einfluss der gross
Industrie auf die Formung
unserer Zeit' [The influence
of heavy industry on the
shaping of our time], *Die
Form*, Berlin 1925, p.234.

The magic some saw in
machines is suggested by
the use of this powered
circular saw as a
textual embellishment.
Riemerschmid, was a
founder-member of the
Deutscher Werkbund,
an association founded
in 1907 with the aim of
uniting artists, craftworkers
and industrialists to work
towards better design
of German products.
Increasingly it lent
towards standardised
machine production.

severe form and rectilinear ornament[35] (Fig. 8). The architect Adolf
Loos (1870-1933), in his celebrated article 'Ornament and crime'
of 1908, went so far as to link the development of culture with the
removal of ornament from articles in daily use, a characteristic
common to the uncluttered functionalist 'look'.[36] Even those
who, like the mystic Paul Scheerbart writing in 1914, found 'the
undecorated "functional style" [*Sachstil*]...inartistic' felt it had merit
for a transition period on the grounds that it had 'done away with
imitations of older styles'.[37]

The sense that design had gone wrong was accompanied by a
conscious search for a new style which was not derived from the
past and was appropropriate to modern life. Kolomon Moser
(1868-1918), the painter-designer who, with the architect–designer
Josef Hoffmann (1870-1956) set up the Wiener Werkstätte, wrote:
'We are now living in the times of automobiles: electric cars, bicycles
and railways. What was good style in stagecoach days is not so now,
what may have been practical then is not so now, and as the times
are, so must art be'.[38] Gropius expressed a similar sentiment in 1913.
'Rococo and Renaissance styles just will not do for the functional
rigour of our modern world...The new times demand their own
expression. The modern architect must develop his aesthetic repertoire
from forms stamped with precision, with nothing left to chance...'.[39]

That a functionalist aesthetic was felt to be especially appropriate to
design in the new century was due partly to an elision of thought
which associated the idea of 'function' with things that functioned,
i.e. machines, so that rooms with functions, especially when they

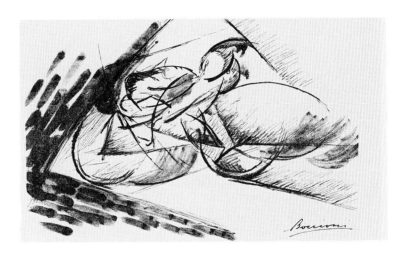

12-13. Two works of art which suggest the romantic attraction machines held for artists early in the twentieth century:

12. 'Minesweepers in port' by Edward Wadsworth (British, 1889-1949), 1918. Woodcut. 5 x 13.6 cm. E.3303 – 1980

Machines not only form the subject matter of this print but are portrayed in a vocabulary derived from their constituent parts: spindles, shafts and cogs.

13. 'Schnelligkeit' [Speed] by Umberto Boccioni (Italian, 1882-1916), about 1914. Plate 2 of album iv in the series *Neue europäische Graphik*, published by the Staatliche Bauhaus, Weimar 1921-3. Lithograph. 28.5 x 38.4 cm. E.40 – 1961

The artist uses a machine capable of speed to create a visual metaphor for speed. Speed expressed through imagery such as this or through ornament as in streamlining is a common characteristic of the formal language of the twentieth century.

made use of new technology, became a significant new site for statements about taste in the home. The diplomat and writer Hermann Muthesius, for example, writing about the modern bathroom concluded that 'Form which has evolved exclusively out of purpose is in itself so ingenious and expressive that it brings an aesthetic satisfaction that differs not at all from artistic enjoyment. We have here an entirely new art…based on actual modern conditions and modern achievements that perhaps one day, when all the fashions that parade as modern movements in art have passed away will be regarded as the most eloquent expression of our age'[40] (Fig. 10).

Machines impinged in a new way on everyday life and were thought to be beautiful partly because they appeared from some viewpoints to have the capacity to make life beautiful. For example much of the beauty perceived in the new kitchen, a twentieth-century concept, arises from its labour-saving nature. Machines presented an infinite range of possibilities which combined greater productivity with greater leisure for working people (Fig. 14). As early as 1901 the influential American architect, Frank Lloyd Wright (1867-1959), while denigrating the actual influence of the machine, asked had it not 'finally made for the artist, whether he will yet own it or not, a splendid distinction between the Art of old and the Art to come? A distinction made by the tool which frees human labor, lengthens and broadens the life of the simplest man, and thereby the basis of the Democracy upon which we insist.'[41] The machine also promised to make possible that which had always seemed impossible. According to the Dutch painter, theorist, and editor of *De Stijl* magazine, Theo van Doesburg (1883-1931), in a lecture given in Berlin, Jena and at the Weimar Bauhaus in 1921: 'All that we used to designate as Magic, Spirit, Love, etc. will now be efficiently accomplished. The idea of the Miraculous, that primitive man made so free with, will now be realised simply through electric current, mechanical control of light and water, the technological conquest of space and time.'[42]

As machines were identified as products belonging especially to the modern world, they were felt to be particularly characteristic of it. Hence, ironically, as the debate concerning the appropriate uses of mechanised production was played out, a style associated with the machine was identified as holding the key to an intrinsically modern style. As the Italian architect Antonio Sant'Elia (1888-1916), a member of the Futurist movement which embraced all the arts in its search for a new art form in tune with contemporary living conditions, wrote in 1914: 'just as the ancients drew inspiration for their art from the elements of nature, so we – who are materially and spiritually artificial – must find this inspiration in the elements of this totally new mechanical world we have created…'.[43] The way in which this inspiration was interpreted and made manifest had many permutations.

Machines themselves, the architecture of industry, and machine-made products were during the first decades of the twentieth century the subjects of romance and exultation (Figs. 11-13). The Futurists extolled the speeding automobile as surpassing the beauty

14. 'Gone the 8-hour day.' Advertisement for Premier Duplex vacuum cleaner in *Woman's home companion*, Ohio, USA, October 1926, p.196

The beauty of this machine lay in the leisure it brought to the housewife who is shown dressed-up and ready to go out.

15. Page from 'Automobiles', *L'esprit nouveau*, Paris 1921, p.1141, later appearing in *Vers une architecture*, Paris 1923.

Le Corbusier argued for a rational aesthetic based on standards established by experiment. Here he presents the Parthenon and the motor-car as 'two products of selection in different fields, one of which has reached its climax and the other is evolving'.

Cliché Albert Morancé.   PARTHÉNON, *de* 447 à 434 *av. J.-C.*

Le standart est une nécessité .

Le standart s'établit sur des bases certaines, non pas arbitrairement, mais avec la sécurité des choses motivées et d'une logique contrôlée par l'expérimentation.

Tous les hommes ont même organisme, mêmes fonctions.

Tous les hommes ont mêmes besoins.

Le contrat social qui évolue à travers les âges détermine des classes, des fonctions, des besoins standarts donnant des produits d'usage standart.

La maison est un produit nécessaire à l'homme.

DELAGE, *Grand-Sport* 1921.

of the 'Victory of Samothrace'[44]. Gropius compared 'The compelling monumentality' of 'the Canadian and South African grain silos, the coal silos built for large railway companies, and the totally modern workshops of the North American firms'[45] with that of the buildings of Ancient Egypt. The French artist, Fernand Léger (1881-1955), whose paintings took abstracted elements of the machine and heroised the human mechanic, claimed that thirty out of a hundred machine-made objects were beautiful compared with only two out of a thousand pictures.[46]

Part of the beauty of modern machines was thought to lie in functionalist principles underlying their forms, in other words that they provided supreme examples of form following function. This was expressed clearly in an article on *The beauty of machines* by Kurt Ewald published in 1925-6. He wrote that they 'are built on purely functional lines, with the purpose of achieving a given performance with the most economical – which means the most perfect – means';[47] and the Constructivists were attracted to their 'simplicity and logic'.[48] That domestic appliances were by 1927, at least, valued as objects of aesthetic value independent of their performance is suggested by the attitude of the Dutch architect-designer, Mart Stam (1899-1986) in his musings on the needs of people in working-class dwellings: 'If pushed they can live without machines to cut their bread and make macaroni or clean their boots, however beautiful these inventions may be'.[49]

The belief was that if similar principles of construction were followed in the design of other products, they would, like machines, be beautiful. Le Corbusier (Charles Edouard Jeanneret 1887-1965), for example, argued 'if houses were constructed by industrial mass-production, like chassis, unexpected but sane and defensible forms would soon appear, and a new aesthetic would be formulated with astonishing precision'[50] (Fig. 15).

The influence of machines was not, however, purely concerned with the principles of their construction and ensuing aesthetic qualities. Machines themselves, and the mass-production of which they are capable, were also valued by artists and designers, particularly

16. MT8. Table lamp designed by Wilhelm Wagenfeld (German, 1900-1990) and made in the Bauhaus workshops, Weimar, Germany, 1924. Nickel-plated brass and milk coloured glass. Height: 35.5 cm. M.28 – 1989

The lamp's title suggests impersonal, standardised mass-production, a much hoped-for aim of Bauhaus designers. Large-scale production was not realised in this case.

17. Chaise-longue designed by Le Corbusier (Charles Edouard Jeanneret, Swiss, 1887-1965), Pierre Jeanneret (Swiss, 1896-1967) and Charlotte Perriand (French, b.1903) and made by Gebrüder Thonet, Frankenberg, Germany, about 1929. Chrome-plated tubular steel, painted sheet steel, animal hide and reinforced rubber. Length: 170cm. W.11 – 1989

This design alludes to machines in several ways. Like them it has movable parts and, in addition, its H-shaped base recalls in its elliptical section the aerodynamically-designed wing struts of Farman aeroplanes, reproduced by Le Corbusier in *Vers une architecture*, Paris 1923, Frederick Etchells, trans. 1927, pp.101-109.

on the left, for ideological reasons.[51] According to the Hungarian sculptor, László Moholy-Nagy (1895-1946) (Fig. 19), 'master of form' at the Bauhaus from 1923-28: 'Before the machine, everyone is equal – I can use it, so can you – it can crush me and the same can happen to you. There is no tradition in technology, no consciousness of class or standing. Everybody can be the machine's master or its slave...This is our century – technology, machines, socialism...it is our task to carry the revolution towards reformation, to fight for a new spirit to fill the forms stamped out by the monstrous machine.'[52] Mass-production, however, while a central tenet of the creators of the Modern Movement, remained largely an aspiration in the early years. For example, although Bauhaus products were understood as industrial forms, most were in fact produced by hand in the Bauhaus's own workshops (Fig. 16) and the furniture designed by Le Corbusier was complicated in terms of construction and therefore required considerable hand-assembly (Fig. 17).

One aspect of the machine's equalising power when used as a means of production lay in the nature of the surface quality it gave. In the words of the Constructivists: 'Hand-made forms contain the graphological biases, characteristic for individual artists; a mechanical performance offers an absolute objectivism of form'.[53] Whether machine-made forms are more objective than their hand-made counterparts is open to question. Part of their perceived objectiveness lay in the impersonality achieved through the use only of ornament intrinsic to the method of construction, as in woven rather than printed textiles (Fig. 23), or to the materials favoured by the Modern

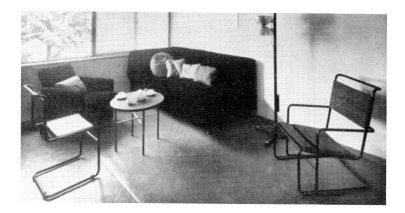

18. Interior of the house designed by Mart Stam (Dutch, 1899–1986) at the Deutscher Werkbund exhibition of 'Die Wohnung' [The Dwelling] in the grounds of the Weissenhof estate, Stuttgart, from *Die Form*, Berlin 1927, p.291.

Stam's first essay on the cantilevered chair involved the use of routine engineering supplies: gas pipes and standard pipe fittings. These examples, however, made by L&C Arnold GmbH, Schorndorf, Germany, were of rigid steel.

Movement, for example chromium-plated steel, marble or glass. Certainly the exclusion of the maker's touch removes a characteristic of form which is capable of exploitation to pander to privilege.[54]

Mass-production, and the anonymity and standardisation it encourages, were in tune with both the socialist drive towards a well-designed environment for all and the international movement towards universal properties in form-giving. Part of Le Corbusier's rationale for the standard type was that 'All men have the same organism, the same functions...the same needs'.[55] Indeed it is in this context that something bordering on a distinctively Modern Movement interpretation of 'form follows function' is realised. Le Corbusier argued: 'The establishment of a standard involves exhausting every practical and reasonable possibility, and extracting from them a recognised type conformable to its functions, with a maximum output and a minimum use of means, workmanship and material, words, forms, colours, sounds'.[56] Die Wohnung [The Dwelling] exhibition held at Stuttgart in 1927, master-minded by the German architect, Ludwig Mies van der Rohe (1886-1969), and including contributions from a wide range of other protagonists of the Modern Movement, was believed to provide examples of this approach (Figs. 18 and 38). The critic, Willi Lotz, in a review of the furniture wrote: 'Objects which are designed not for the sake of appearance but to fulfil their function as well as possible, will arrive at that form which most clearly expresses that function. The aim set by our generation is to make form an expression of function, not

19. László Moholy-Nagy (Hungarian, 1895-1946) photographed at the Bauhaus by Lucia Moholy (Czech, b.1894), 1925. Bauhaus Archiv, Berlin

The sculptor, Moholy-Nagy, 'master of form' at the Bauhaus from 1923 to 1928, wore workman's overalls to reinforce his vision of the designer as technician.

20. Armchairs designed by Gerrit Rietveld (Dutch, 1888-1964), 1918 and made by Rietveld assisted by G. van der Groenekan, Netherlands, c.1920 and c.1923. Stained sycamore and sycamore plywood; painted beech and beech plywood. Heights: 89 and 87 cm. W.9 – 1989 and The Centraal Museum, Utrecht

A comparison between these two versions of this significant chair emphasises the extent to which its design acted as an opportunity to study the abstract interaction of rectangles, solid and void, in space. The number of members in the later version is reduced and their dimensions subtly altered.

the expression of a self-justifying aesthetic…'.[57] However, any suggestion that herein lay the recipe for definitive form was qualified by both Le Corbusier and Lotz. The former asked for 'a perfection and harmony beyond the mere practical'[58] and the latter stated that: 'no one would maintain that *the* chair or *the* bed could ever be finally constructed or that it will actually emerge from a process of natural selection. For if there were such a thing as *the* definitive form, it could only be for a specific period of time and in a specific material…'[59]

Moreover, only rarely was it claimed that there was a causal relationship between function and beauty, or even that functional form was a valid alternative to beautiful form. Tim Benton has pointed out that in British writing from 1927 to 1939 Le Corbusier was invariably referred to as a functionalist.[60] The architect's description of the house as a machine for living in, and beds and chairs as resting machines must have contributed to this. But he was also an architect who not only allowed a tree to grow through the middle of his famous Pavillon de l'Esprit Nouveau at the Paris Exhibition of 1925 but was also an abstract painter of considerable standing. In fact an attentive reading of Le Corbusier's writings makes it clear that he did not equate functional form with beauty: 'When a thing responds to a need, it is not beautiful; it satisfies all one part of our mind, the primary part, without which there is no possibility of richer satisfactions'[61] or to take a more rapturous passage: 'You employ stone, wood and concrete, and with these materials you

21-24. Four images which provide the opportunity to explore the use of geometric form by the Modern Movement:

build houses and palaces. That is construction. Ingenuity is at work. But suddenly you touch my heart, you do me good, I am happy and I say: "This is beautiful". That is Architecture. Art enters in. My house is practical. I thank you, as I might thank Railway engineers, or the Telephone service. You have not touched my heart. But suppose that walls rise towards heaven in such a way that I am moved…These shapes are such that they are clearly revealed in light. The relationships between them have not necessarily any reference to what is practical or descriptive…By the use of raw materials and *starting from* conditions more or less utilitarian, you have established certain relationships which have aroused my emotions'.[62] Considerable emphasis has been put on the attention he gave to industrial buildings and machines in *Vers une architecture* but in fact views of earlier architecture outnumber those of grain silos, cars and aeroplanes added together (Fig. 15). It can be argued that the critical concentration on this aspect of his thought was all part of the magic that machines held at the time or the threat they posed, depending on your viewpoint.

The forms favoured by Le Corbusier were the primary forms identified by ancient geometry: 'cubes, cones, spheres, cylinders or pyramids' on the grounds that 'the image of these is distinct and tangible within us and without ambiguity. It is for that reason that these are *beautiful forms, the most beautiful forms.*'[63] This statement leaves us in no doubt that their attraction lay in their formal impact rather than in any link the form has to utility.

Elementary form was fundamental to the creativity of other adherents of the Modern Movement. Van Doesburg's magazine, *De Stijl*, which began publication in 1917, was originally to have been titled 'The straight line', and the vertical and horizontal are paramount in the work of all members of the De Stijl group. In his revolutionary and influential design for an armchair, Gerrit Rietveld (1888-1964) limits his vocabulary to the rectangle. The component parts of the chair are broken down into pure structure: the arms and legs treated as a grid, the seat and back as planes. Clearly he was more concerned with analysing the components of the chair than with the provision of comfort (Fig. 20).

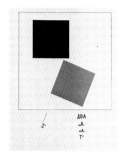

21. Page from El Lissitsky, *Suprematicheskii skaz: pro dva kvadrata v 6-ti postroikakh* [The Suprematist tale: two squares in 6 constructions], Berlin 1922.

This experimental children's book tells of the struggle for power between the red (the lower square) and the black square.

22. Ashtray designed and made by Marianne Brandt (German, 1893-1983) in the Bauhaus metal workshop, Weimar, 1923-4. Brass and nickel silver alloy. Height: 6.7 cm. M.73 – 1988

Brandt joined the Bauhaus when László Moholy-Nagy was re-organising the metal workshop into a research centre for industrial prototype production. Her designs of elementary forms expressed the idea of modernity, although they were still handmade.

23.'Damast.' Wall-hanging designed and woven by Gunta Stölzl (German, 1897-1983) at the Dessau Bauhaus, Germany, 1926-27. Hand jacquard woven silk and cotton. 130 x 73.5 cm. Circ.709 – 1967

The anti-ornament programme of the Bauhaus restricted textile production to weaving. Thus any pattern was an integral part of the object and thus of its form.

The square, the circle and the triangle, referred to by Paul Klee (1879-1940), Swiss painter and Master at the Bauhaus from 1921 to 1931, as the three basic forms,[64] were also characteristic leitmotivs of Bauhaus production (Figs. 22-4). The painter Johannes Itten (1888-1967), however, made it clear in a 1917 diary entry that they were for him of emotional rather than functional significance: 'to the spiritually aware these three symbols are not hollow forms but embody the most powerful forces of creation';[65] when Master of the Preliminary Course at the Bauhaus from 1919 to 1921, he claimed later to have 'made [the students] stand up and make circles with their arms until at last the entire body had entered into a relaxed swinging motion'.[66] Factions are said to have arisen within the Bauhaus arguing about which was the most beautiful form of all.

An analysis of the 'functional' aspects of Modernist design need not only point to the formal vocabulary as independent of the aesthetic. Buckminster Fuller (1895-1983), the American architect and engineer, famous for his Geodesic Domes, structures based on octahedrons and tetrahedrons, gave this appraisal: 'The 'International Style' brought to America by the Bauhaus innovators...was but super-ficial. It peeled off yesterday's exterior embellishment and put on instead formalised novelties of quasi-simplicity, permitted by the same hidden structural elements of modern alloys that had permitted the discarded *Beaux-Arts* garmentation...the Bauhaus and International used standard plumbing fixtures and only ventured so far as to persuade manufacturers to modify the surface of the valve handles and spigots, and the colour, size, and arrangements of the tiles. The International Bauhaus never went back of the wall-surface to look at the plumbing...they never enquired into the overall problem of sanitary fittings themselves...In short they only looked at problems of modifications of the surface of end-products, which end-products were inherently sub-functions of a technically obsolete world.'[67] Reyner Banham has pointed out that Le Corbusier did not, as had Buckminster Fuller in his unrealised Dymaxion House project of 1927 (Fig. 26), rethink the plan of a house so that its mechanical elements were centralised.[68]

One answer to the question posed at the beginning of this section is

24. Room in the Moholy-Nagys' house at the Bauhaus, Dessau, photographed by Lucia Moholy (Czech, b.1894), from *Das Werk*, Berlin 1928, p.9.

The house was designed by Walter Gropius (German, 1883-1969), the furniture by Marcel Breuer (Hungarian, 1902-1981), the light by Marianne Brandt (German, 1893-1983) and the painting by László Moholy-Nagy (Hungarian, 1895-1946) himself. The designs show a fascination with elemental geometric form.

MODERN CARPET DESIGNS MAY PROVIDE END-LESS ENTERTAINMENT FOR YOUR FRIENDS

25. 'Modern carpet designs may provide endless entertainment for your friends.' Illustration to Heath Robinson and K.R.G.Browne, *How to live in a flat*, London 1936, p.43.

A joke at the expense of the fashion for geometric form.

that functional form as realised by protagonists of the Modern Movement was as much a styling feature as say the flutes and friezes of Neo-classicism and the shell-like ornamentation of the Rococo. Some who were not fully committed to Modernism saw this at the time. The French interior decorator and founding director of the design studio of Galeries Lafayette department store, Maurice Dufrêne (1876-1955), described it as 'the universal cult of "nothing" …a fashion itself, and like all fashions the fashion for "nothing" will pass'.[69] And at about the same time, John Betjeman, the future

26. Plan and elevation of
the minimum Dymaxion
House, 1927-9 by Richard
Buckminster Fuller
(USA, 1895-1983).
Jonathan Cape

This never-realised
house constituted a
radical rethinking of the
plan and construction of
the home. Services were
to be housed in a central
mast to which each spatial
unit was to be independently
related, thus facilitating
their replacement when
more desirable units were
developed. Beds and
seating were to be
pneumatic.

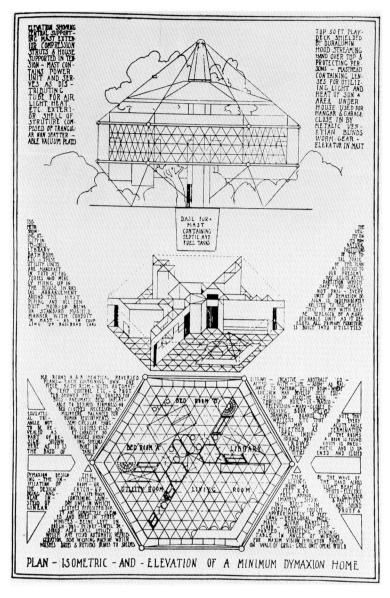

British Poet Laureate, when Assistant Editor of the *Architectural Review*, lampooned his circle as:

'…functional folk who like beauty stark
And decorate our rooms with it in Belsize Park'.[70]

It can be argued that functional form was as symbolic and associative as form at any period. The Dessau Bauhaus was designed with a road running through it (Fig. 27) not because it was a functional

27. The Bauhaus, Dessau, nearing completion, designed by Walter Gropius (German, 1883-1969), photographed by Lucia Moholy (Czech, b.1894), from *Das Werk*, Berlin 1928, p.5.

The form of the building is based on variations of the cube with different functions ascribed to the differentiated blocks: student accommodation, workshops, the Dessau trade school, and administration and architecture. The design expressed visually as well as in use the value the Bauhaus attached to a particular kind of organisational functionalism.

requirement but as a symbol of the school's progressive attitude. What the 'functional' style signified was economical and 'progressive' efficiency at every stage in an object's life: tooling, production, packaging, marketing and use. Surely the Hungarian designer, Marcel Breuer (1902-1981), used metal in his furniture not as he claimed because it was styleless but rather because its associations with industry contributed to an image of the domestic interior as 'nothing but a necessary apparatus for contemporary life'[71] (Fig. 28). The design of the Modern house and its contents was intended to suggest that it ran with the efficiency of the idealised machine responding to domestic needs as the laboratory responds to those of the scientist.

28. Cover for *Breuer Metallmöbel*, a catalogue of tubular steel furniture designed by Marcel Breuer (Hungarian, 1902-1981) with typography by Herbert Bayer (Austrian, 1900-1985) and photographed by Erich Consemüller, Dessau c.1927. E.1483 – 1981

Breuer's interest in tubular steel was given impetus by the purchase of his first bicycle in 1925. The use here of a negative image, itself a sign of the fascination of technology, suggested by association that the wares for sale within were also the products of technological achievement.

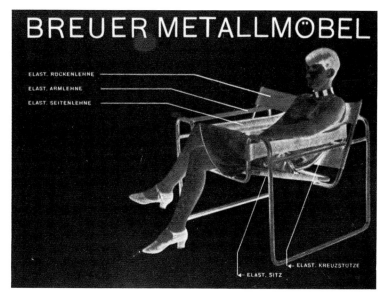

BREUER METALLMÖBEL

ELAST. RÜCKENLEHNE
ELAST. ARMLEHNE
ELAST. SEITENLEHNE

← ELAST. KREUZSTÜTZE
← ELAST. SITZ

29. The workshop wing of the Bauhaus, Dessau, photographed by Lucia Moholy (Czech, b.1894) from *Documents internationaux de l'esprit nouveau*, no.1, Paris c.1927, p.24.

The Bauhaus is a magnificent example of the cantilever structure, made possible by the development of reinforced concrete. The glass curtain wraps around the load-bearing members allowing a clear view into and out of the workshops. This striking perspective view suggests that it had for the photographer an inspirational quality also.

Form and Process

Frank Lloyd Wright, writing in 1928 on the *Meaning of material*, likened the architect's materials to the painter's palette: 'Each material has its own message and, to the creative artist, its song...Each material *speaks a language* of its own just as line and colour speak ...Each has a story'.[72] The maxim 'form follows function' suggests that function should be the decisive factor in the creation of form but in reality it is, and should be dependent on many factors including the materials used to 'form' it and the method used to 'form' them.

Clearly different materials have different characteristics in a variety of different combinations: they may, for example, be hard or soft, rigid or flexible, opaque or transparent, more or less absorbent, a conductor or not of heat; they are capable of bearing different kinds of stresses and accepting different kinds of finishes; they can also be worked in a multitude of different ways. Equally clearly, in the words of the Polish painter Mieczyslan Szczuka (1898-1927) and of T. Zarnower, investigating the nature of Constructivism:[73] 'The properties of the created thing must *depend* upon the employed material. Constructional merits of the material – the types of its surface – its colours – its different surface properties as dependent on the finish – its peculiarities when exposed to light etc.'[74] Moreover the properties of, say, glass are not only different from those of, say, wood, but those of blown glass are different from those of, for example, moulded glass.

The idea that form should respect the characteristics of the material out of which it is formed has, like the message of Sullivan's maxim, been a staple of Western design theory, also traceable to Vitruvius[75] and reiterated with similar frequency thereafter. Popularised with the words 'truth to materials', paraphrased from the writings of, among others, the theorist John Ruskin[76] and the designer William Morris (1834-1896),[77] it has formed a refrain with 'form follows function' in twentieth-century texts on design and, arguably, played an even more fundamental part in how design has been taught.

30-32 Three chairs, designed by different Italian designers in the late 1960s, which explore the formal qualities of different plastics:

30. 'Blow.' Chair designed by Carla Scolari, Donato D'Urbino, Paolo Lomazzi and Gionatan de Pas (all Italian, b.1930s), and made by Zanotta Poltrona, Milan, Italy, 1967. PVC film seam-welded by radio frequency. Height: 84 cm. Circ.100 – 1970

The introduction of high-frequency welding of PVC in the mid-1960s stimulated interest in inflatable structures. This was the first mass-produced totally inflatable chair.

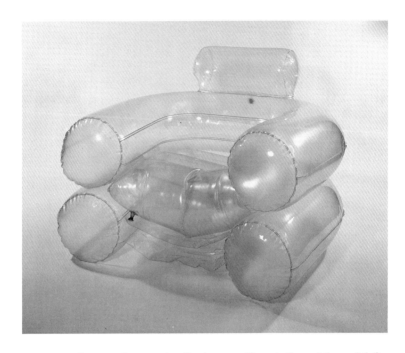

For example a student at the Bauhaus, still an influential model for design education throughout Europe and the USA, described the first day of the preliminary course at the school thus: 'Josef Albers[78] entered the room with a bundle of newspapers under one arm, which he gave out to the students. He then turned to us with roughly the following words: "Ladies and gentlemen…Every work of art starts from a specific material, and we must therefore first study how that material is constituted…The complexity of the form is dependent on the material with which we are working…I would now like you to take the newspaper you have just been given and make something out of it which is more than it is now. I would also like you to respect the material, employ it in a meaningful way and thereby consider its characteristic qualities."…Hours later he returned, and…picked out one very simple-looking piece of work by a young Hungarian architect. He had done nothing more than fold the material from top to bottom so that it stood up like a pair of wings. Josef Albers now explained how well the material had been understood, how well it had been used and how folding was a particularly appropriate process to apply to paper since it made what was such a soft material rigid, indeed so rigid that it could be stood on its narrowest point – its edge.'[79] After paper the students worked first with glass and then with metal before they were free to experiment with materials of their choice. Such an emphasis on material and technique has inevitably influenced how the activity of design is approached and concomitantly the form of the end-product.

Respect for the formal characteristics inherent in materials has been combined in the twentieth century with a belief that new materials hold the key to new forms. Adolf Loos writing disapprovingly in 1898 of the use of cement, a rediscovery of the nineteenth century, cast into consoles, festoons and cartouches in emulation of stone and 'nailed on' the buildings around the Ring in his adopted city, Vienna, insisted that a technique should not be used to create 'forms which are specifically related to another material simply because no practical difficulties stand in the way. The artist's duty must always be to find new plastic language for new materials.'[80] These thoughts have frequently been echoed throughout the century. The American designer, Donald Dohner, employed by the Westinghouse Company particularly associated in the 1930s with electrical appliances, argued in an article of 1937 on the 'Technique of designing': 'Imitating other materials may be an interesting technical stunt for some engineer but it robs the new material of its birthright, destroys its identity and natural beauty, thereby degrading

31. 'Sacco.' Chair designed by Piero Gatti, Cesare Paolini and Franco Teodoro (all Italian, b. c.1940) and made by Zanotta, Milan, Italy, 1968-9. Expanded polystyrene granules, skinflex cover. Height: 128 cm. Circ.73 – 1970

This amorphous chair, a bag half-filled with plastic granules which adapt to the shape of the body on contact and yet are firm, changes its shape to accommodate that of the sitter.

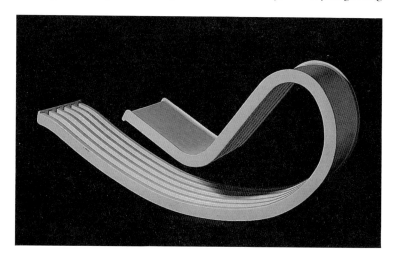

32. Rocking chair designed by Cesare Leonardi (Italian, b.1935) and Franca Stagi (Italian, b.1937) and made by Elco, Venice, Italy, 1967. Moulded fibre glass Height: 85 cm. Circ.329 – 1970

This chair, shown at the International Furniture Exhibition at Milan in 1968, uses the characteristics of moulded fibre glass to create a re-thinking of the traditional rocker. Its single, looping form of sculptural perfection both expresses and serves its purpose.

33. Kitchen at the Stockholm Exhibition, 1930. Svensk Form

This exhibition was the first to promote the use of stainless steel for kitchen surfaces. The availability of sheet metal, which has so influenced the appearance of twentieth-century products, is dependent on the existence of heavy industrial machines to produce it. The inherent antiseptic nature of its unabsorbent smoothness has encouraged a clean aesthetic as well as facilitating actual cleanliness.

it'.[81] Similarly the Danish architect and designer, Verner Panton (b.1926), explaining his approach to design in 1969, said: 'I try to forget existing examples…and concern myself above all with the material. The result then rarely has four legs, not because I do not wish to make such a chair, but because the processing of materials like wire or polyester calls for new shapes'[82] (Fig. 47). Equally it was felt that new means of production should lead to new forms. Gregor Paulsson, secretary of the Svenska Slöjdföreningen [the

Swedish Society of Craft and Industrial Design, now known as Svensk Form], for example, argued in his book *Vackrare Vardagsvara* [More Beautiful Everyday Goods], published in 1919: 'Now that we have the machines let us, instead of imitating form, products and techniques, try to design goods that are characteristic of machine production...Let us, with the help of these technical aids, produce the new.'[83]

In practice many of the materials associated with twentieth-century form, especially in terms of architecture, were not in fact inventions of it. Iron dates back to pre-historic times, glass to ancient Egypt and concrete to ancient Rome. Changes in the production of these materials had by the twentieth century, however, greatly extended their potential in use.[84]

The industrialisation of iron's production in the second half of the eighteenth century meant that it was produced in great enough quantity to become viable as a building material; this made possible the creation of structures with a greater span than ever before. New possibilities were also opened up by the exploitation of steel, an alloy of iron, with much greater strength and malleability; and its uses were subsequently extended in 1840 by the advent of electro-plating which showed the way for its protection from rust by the application of a thin coating of rust-proof material. Without these developments the tubular-steel chromium nickel-plated furniture associated with the Modernists could not have been manufactured.

The embedding of steel rods in concrete by French engineers in the 1890s also made possible an entirely new approach to construction. Indeed walls were no longer needed to hold up the floors above, which in turn made possible a completely new kind of spatial organisation. In the words of the Los Angeles-based architect, Rudolf M. Schindler (1887-1953), it made 'The twentieth century... the first to abandon construction as a source of architectural form'.[85]

Developments in the manufacture of glass in the second half of the nineteenth century allowed sheets of much greater size to be produced. The potential of the material was so altered that Frank Lloyd Wright singled it out as the material most distinctive of his

34. Lounge Chair model LCW, designed by Charles Eames (USA, 1907-1978) and Ray Eames (USA, 1916?-1988) 1945-6 and made by Evans Products Co., Los Angeles, USA, about 1947. Height: 73 cm. W.17 – 1989

This chair, consisting of five complex moulded wood parts, used technology the Eames encountered during their wartime commission to develop leg splints, stretchers, and glider shells. Its organic form, however, appears to foreshadow those which the emergence of different plastics made so much easier to achieve (e.g. Figs 45-47).

time: 'Perhaps the greatest difference eventually between ancient and modern buildings will be due to our modern machine-made glass. Glass, in any wide utilitarian sense, is new'.[86] Its use in combination with reinforced concrete meant that for the first time it was possible for the exterior of a building to consist of a skin of glass rather than a solid wall pierced by windows (Fig. 29).

The century has, of course, also seen the introduction of materials which are totally new. The largest and most significant group for the purposes of this study is the majority of those known as plastics. These are materials softened by heat and moulded in the course of their manufacture, some retaining the ability to turn pliable in heat and others setting for ever. The material can be natural, such as rubber or horn, but increasingly the term has come to be associated with synthetic materials of which the first was Bakelite, discovered in 1907. There is now a great variety of plastics to which others are constantly being added. As each is the result of a different chemical formulation, each has different characteristics and thus different possibilities in terms of form which have been adventurously exploited by the design industry since the middle of the century[87] (Figs. 30-2).

Not only has the evolution of materials played a part in the creation of form but also the availability of new ways of processing them. The introduction of steel-stamping machinery, essential for the production of the flat plates of thin-pressed, enamelled steel which became such a feature of the 'flushed-off' kitchens of the 1930s (Fig. 33), did more than make possible the production of steel-cased household machinery; the need to see a good return on the investment the machinery involved actually encouraged its production.[88] Equally advancements in the moulding of plywood developed for its use in aircraft construction in the First World War enabled the Finnish architect-designer, Alvar Aalto, to mass-produce plywood furniture, a process which Michael Thonet (1796–1871) had not mastered; further elaboration of the process enabled plywood to take up the complex curves in more than one plane which became increasingly popular in a range of materials in the 1950s[89] (Fig. 34). The invention of a portable furnace by Dominick Labino, a glass technician who developed the silica-fibre panels that cover the surface of Nasa space shuttles, meant that from 1964 onwards miniature glass workshops could be set up in private studios; this has resulted in a great expansion in the production of the wondrous translucent creations known as 'art' glass.

Technical advances in the working parts of products have also influenced the form of many of them. A simple example is the effect of the development of transistors in the 1950s, followed by the microchip in the 1980s. They have made possible such an extreme reduction in the size of among other products radios and calculators that the previously heavy and cumbersome has not only become easily portable but capable, even, of resembling a credit card. Miniature components have also made possible the creation of new products. The potential of the technology has become expressed in form through a fashion for miniaturisation (Figs. 35–37).

The influence of the microchip has been even more pervasive in terms of production. The part played in the nineteenth century by mechanisation in encouraging the limitation of form and ornamentation to that which could be mass-produced easily and thus economically has already been mentioned.[90] Re-programmable computer-driven tools which have made shorter production runs economical are now reversing this trend and encouraging the production of a wealth of different runs of similar but differentiated products as in the case of Swatch watches or Nike trainers (Fig. 63).

None of these developments, however, whether concerned with

37. Sinclair microvision television, designed and made by Sinclair Radionics Ltd., St Ives, Britain, 1977. Plastic and electronic components.
Science Museum (by courtesy of the Board of Trustees) no.1978-137

The miniaturisation made possible by new technology has led to its exploration even where, as here, its practicality can be questioned: the tiny screen is not easy to view. Yet, marketed as 'the only pocket television anywhere in the world', 4000 sets were being made a month by the end of the first year of production.

38-39. Building projects which demonstrate the capacity of reinforced concrete to create different architectural form:

38. View of houses by Walter Gropius (German 1883-1969), Le Corbusier (Charles Edouard Jeanneret, Swiss, 1887-1965) and J.J.P.Oud (Dutch, 1890-1963) at the Deutscher Werkbund exhibition of 'Die Wohning' [The Dwelling] in the grounds of the Weissenhof estate, Stuttgart, from *Die Form*, Berlin 1927, p.259.

The designs of these houses by three different architects from three different countries are all essays on the square and the cube, forms favoured by the Modern Movement.

material, technique or working parts has normally imposed form. Many materials can take on a wealth of different forms naturally. In their early days synthetic plastics were notorious for taking the forms associated with natural materials, for example tortoise-shell and ivory, or, indeed, wood; and reinforced concrete is as equally suited to the crisp elementary forms favoured by the first generation of Modernists (Fig. 38) as to the organic forms of, say, Eero Saarinen's (1910-1961) TWA Terminal at Idlewild (now JFK) airport (Fig. 39). Even when, as in the case of inflated plastics, the material and technique do dictate a certain quality of form, be the product a chair (Fig. 30) or a building (Fig. 40), there remains the option not to use them in the first place.

The pervasiveness of a particular type of form at any period across a huge range of materials, suggests that form frequently evolves independently of material and technique (Figs. 41 and 42). What, however, they do undoubtedly contribute is a range of possibilities, even suggestions, which, just like the function a product is to fulfil, contain within them inspiration.

This inspiration may derive from their visual qualities. Le Corbusier stated, when comparing the purity of form and faultless surface of

39. TWA Terminal at Idlewild (now JFK) airport, New York, USA, designed by Eero Saarinen and Associates, 1956-62. Yale University Press

The architect, Eero Saarinen (USA, 1910-1961) in *Eero Saarinen on his work*, New Haven and London 1962, said of this project: 'The challenge was... One, to create...a building for TWA which would be distinctive and memorable... Two, to design a building in which the architecture itself would express the drama and specialness and excitement of travel'.

40. Fuji Group Pavilion designed by Yutaka Murata (Japanese) and Mamoru Kawaguchi (Japanese) for the World Fair, Osaka, Japan, 1970. PVA-impregnated canvas, insulated with PVC and coated with Du Pont's 'Hypalon' synthetic rubber.

The largest pneumatic structure to date when built, it had a circular plan 50 metres in diameter. It consisted of sixteen air beams anchored around the circumference, each beam 4 metres in diameter, and 72 metres long. The air beams bulged higher where their ends were closer together.

41-42. Scientific imagery, which celebrated the achievements of science and reinforced the promise it seemed to offer, was used in the design of a wide range of products after the Second World War:

41. View of the Atomium, designed by André Polack and André Waterkeyn, from the entrance hall of the Brussels International Exhibition, 1958. Jean Malvaux

Rising 102 metres high, its form was based on an iron molecule magnified over 150 million times. It acted as a symbol for the fair and of the power of Belgian industry.

42. 'Springbok' chair. Designed by Ernest Race (British, 1913-1964) and made by Race Furniture Ltd, Sheerness, 1950. Steel rod frame, stove enamelled, with springs covered in PVC tubing; cast aluminium feet. Height: 79 cm. Design Council

Scientific imagery was an important strand in the 'Festival Style' fostered by the 1951 Festival of Britain.

machine production with the idiosyncracies of hand-crafted goods, that the poet is not assassinated but rather reborn: 'the poet holds a ball of shining steel in his hand and thinks: and this is proof of the God whom I seek'[91]. This suggests the extent to which the gleam of machine-polished steel could inspire him (Fig. 43). Glass is another material by which many designers in the first half of the century were fascinated. The Australian interior designer Raymond McGrath (1903-1977), who worked in Britain, claimed that the passion for glass in the 1930s was not a style or fashion but a spiritual discovery...providing sheets of reflection...as valuable as lakes of water in a formal garden'[92] (Fig. 44).

Equally the inspiration may reside in the physical properties of a material. The British designer Robin Day (b.1915) wrote on the conception of his Polyprop chair: 'The invention of polypropylene seemed to me to offer exciting possibilities for the development of a

43-44. Two images where
the nature of the materials
used are crucial to their
visual impact:

43. Stainless steel bowl
displayed in a kitchen at
the Stockholm Exhibition,
1930. Svensk Form

This anonymous
photographer finds
poetry in the form and
material of this essentially
functional bowl.

44. View in The Glass
Age Exhibition Train
photographed by John
Somerset Murray
(British), 1937.
E.448 – 1947

new chair. Its low cost, great strength, and suitability for injection-moulding made it ideal for a mass-produced one-piece back and seat, which could be mounted on various frame-types for different purposes.' He was also attracted to its 'natural flexibility' as compared with the relative rigidity of glass-fibre reinforced plastic.[93]

The production method itself may also provide an inspirational challenge. Injection-moulding is expensive in terms of tools and moulds but virtually automatic once set up: one shell can be made every ninety seconds. This means that the design must be correct at the tooling stage and there must be a large market for it. The Polyprop chair has met the challenge: thirty years after the first shell was made it is still in production and has been sold in twenty-three different countries (Fig. 45).

The role of materials and techniques is not even limited to what in practical terms they have made possible. Their inspirational power is such that they contain within them aspirations to form which they cannot necessarily deliver. An example is Eero Saarinen's ubiquitous Tulip chair from the Pedestal range which he had intended initially to mould in one piece from glass-fibre reinforced plastic. The material, however, proved not to have sufficient structural strength and consequently the seat was supported on a cast aluminium pedestal, coated in plastic to give the chair the

The Glass Train, consisting
of two converted LNER
coaches, was created by
Kenneth Cheeseman for
Pilkington Brothers Ltd, at
a cost of £3000. It aimed
to show 'what could be
done with contemporary
methods, and to stimulate
imagination regarding the
decorative properties of
different glass products'.
The exhibition travelled
over 2000 miles around
Britain, stopping at 40
different towns, and had
an attendance of 400,000.

45. Polyprop chair, mark II, designed by Robin Day (British, b. 1915), 1962-3; made by S.Hille & Co., Ltd, Britain, from 1963. Injection-moulded polypropylene shell on metal base. Height: 74 cm. Circ.15 – 1966

This was the first chair designed specifically to be made in polypropylene, invented in 1954, and the first chair to be made by injection moulding, a technique subsequently widely used in their mass-production.

46. Chair from the 'Tulip' pedestal range, designed by Eero Saarinen (USA, 1910-1961) and made by Knoll International, East Grenville, USA, 1956-7. Glass fibre shell, aluminium base. Height: 80 cm. Circ. 86 – 1969

In 1958 Saarinen argued that: 'All the great furniture of the past from Tutankhamum's chair to Thomas Chippendale's has always been a structural total. With our excitement over plastic and plywood shells, we grew away from the structural total. As now manufactured, the pedestal furniture is half-plastic, half-metal. I look forward to the day when the plastics industry has advanced to the point where the chair will be one material, as designed.'

visual unity that Saarinen sought (Fig. 46). Indeed the first 'plastic' chair thought to have been successfully moulded in one piece was designed seven years before the facilities to bring it into production were available (Fig. 47). Its designer, Verner Panton, says: 'Steel tubes, foam, springs, and covers have been so developed technically that we can create forms which were unthinkable just a few years ago. Designers should now use these materials to create objects which up to now they could only see in their dreams. Personally,

I'd like to design chairs which exhaust all the technical possibilities of the present in which I also live.'[94]

It is clear that what *has* become possible during the century has awakened the design industry to investigate what *might* become possible as well as having provided greater freedom of choice in form and, thus, a more extensive formal language than hitherto experienced.

47. Stacking chair designed by Verner Panton (Danish, b.1926), 1960, and made by Herman Miller 1967. Fibreglass with polyester resin. Height: 82 cm. Circ.74 – 1969

This was probably the first single-piece chair to be made using an injection moulding process. Its cantileved form shows Panton pushing available technology to its limits. His furniture aimed 'to provoke people into using their imaginations' as much as to fulfil a practical function.

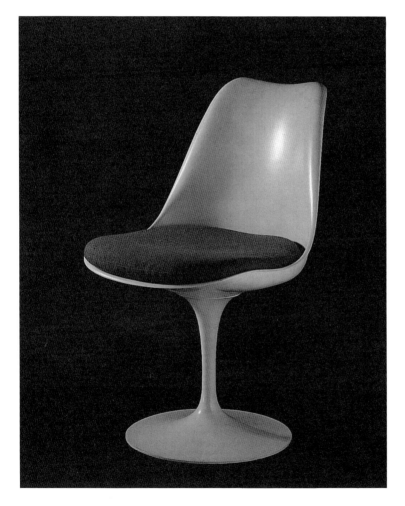

48. Cover of
Time magazine,
31 October 1949.

The appearance of a
portrait of the American
designer, Raymond Loewy
(1883-1986), on the cover
of *Time* magazine suggests
the extent to which design
had entered the American
consciousness. The caption
'He streamlines the sales
curve' alludes to the form
with which he is associated
as well as to its selling
power.

TIME

THE WEEKLY NEWSMAGAZINE

DESIGNER RAYMOND LOEWY
He streamlines the sales curve.

Form and the Design System

Norman Bel Geddes (1893-1952), theatre designer turned industrial design consultant, responsible in 1926 for opening one of the first industrial design offices in the USA, defined design as 'a mental conception of something to be done. A visual design is the organism of an idea of a visual nature so that it may be executed. It is the practice of organising various elements to produce a desired result. Design deals exclusively with organisation and arrangement of form.'[95] Design, according to this definition, has always played a central role in the creation of objects either intuitively or pragmatically. As the production process has become more complicated, and the business of making increasingly separated from decisions concerning the form being made, a profession known as designer especially associated with the form-giving aspects of the process has emerged.

During this century the contribution of the designer has been especially valued. It is not surprising that the architect Walter Gropius, even before he was Director of the Bauhaus, should have stressed its importance: 'The artist has the power to give the lifeless machine-made product a soul, it is his creative force which will live on, actively embodied in its outward form. His collaboration is not just a luxury, generously thrown in as an extra, it is an indispensable part of the industrial process and must be regarded as such…'.[96]

After the collapse of international economics in 1929, it was, however, to design that governments and business alike looked for regeneration. Lord Gorell, Chairman of a Committee of Art and Industry appointed by the British Board of Trade in 1931, said in a talk on the radio: 'Our one desire is to stimulate trade at home and widen our markets abroad…There is only one road to prosperity – namely to call in the artistic resources of the nation.'[97]

It was also precisely during these years of Depression that the industrial designer, a specifically twentieth-century type of designer concerned in the words of another of the profession's first practitioners, Raymond Loewy (1883-1986), with 'lipsticks to locomotives',[98]

49-51. Three products provide an opportunity to investigate the stylistic characteristics of different designers:

49. Wardrobe designed by Ernest Barnsley (British, 1863-1926) and probably made at the Daneway House Workshops, Gloucestershire, 1902. Height: 170 cm. W.39 – 1977

The massive construction, chip-carving, 'exposed' joints and latch closing of this wardrobe are features common in the products of the English Arts and Crafts Movement. Yet the manner in which they come together in this piece is especially characteristic of Barnsley

was identified in the USA, and increasingly awarded the kind of mass-adoration given to film stars. As Loewy reminisced: 'Success finally came when we were able to convince some creative men that a good appearance was a saleable commodity, that it often cut costs, enhanced a product's prestige, raised corporate profits, benefited the customer, and increased employment'[99] (Fig. 48).

Looked at from one point of view it is logical to single out the designer as the inspirational power in form-giving. Just as we can recognise the hand of a painter or sculptor so we can recognise that of a particular designer, be it, for example, through the ruggedly chunky lines of, say, the British Arts and Crafts designer Sidney Barnsley (1863-1926) (Fig. 49), the refined elegant lines of, say, the German industrial designer Dieter Rams (b. 1932) (Fig. 50), or the anarchic whimsy of say the French super-star, Philippe Starck (b.1949) (Fig. 51). If certain forms are characteristic of certain designers, it cannot be denied that they have played a significant part in shaping them.

Equally it is in connection with changes in form that their intervention is most visible in the finished product. The change may be apparently radical as in the provision of casings for machines which had previously shown their working parts like typewriter and sewing machines (Fig. 52) or more subtle as in car styling (Fig. 57).

Designers are, however, dependent on far more people than are painters or sculptors. While you can paint in a garret, hoping posterity will come to appreciate your work, a designer must collaborate with those in business if a design is to have any form as a three-dimensional product. The American designer, Henry Dreyfuss, pointed out that the picture of the 'industrial designer [as] a brisk, suave character, brimming with confidence, who bustles around factories and stores, streamlining stoves and refrigerators that aren't going anywhere, reshaping doorknobs, and squinting at this year's automobiles and arbitarily deciding that next year's fenders should be two or three eighths inches longer' was a caricature. 'Actually…He is a businessman as well as a person who makes drawings and models. He is a keen observer of public taste and he has painstakingly cultivated his own taste. He has an understanding of merchandising, how things are made, packed, distributed, and displayed. He accepts the responsibility of his position as liaison linking the management, engineering, and the consumer and co-operates with all three.'[100]

Design is in practice a circular process in which the designer acts as the broker, any stage of which contributes to the final form of a

50. Shaver. Braun pocket de luxe designed and made by Braun AG, Germany, 1992. Plastic and metal. Height: 11.5 cm. M.24 – 1992

The pebble-like form, which makes this shaver a delight to hold, recurs in a wide range of well-mannered household appliances produced by Braun, where Dieter Rams (German, b.1932) has been director of product design since 1962.

51. Ara. Table lamp designed by Philippe Starck (French, b.1949), made by Flos SpA, Brescia, Italy, 1988. Chrome-plated steel. Height: 56.5 cm. M.16 – 1993

The curved horn is a recurring form in the designs of Philippe Starck, who juxtaposes unexpected shapes and materials to create an individual style which is instantly recognisable. Here movement of the horn switches the light in its head on and off.

product. The influence of process on form was discussed in the previous section. Process can in addition provide the impetus to form. A manufacturer may have equipment standing idle and be looking for a product which will use it (Fig. 53). A supplier of materials may be looking for a product to use them. This was especially the case with plastics' manufacturers after the Second World War (Fig. 54). An entrepreneur may detect a market for a certain sort of product; on the other hand, the consumer, the person who selects one form rather than another, may be the driving force behind the defining of shape.

The lesson learnt by Henry Ford is well-known. Drawing on Adam Smith's theories on mass-production, he founded the Ford Motor Company in 1903, stating his commitment to standardisation: 'The way to make automobiles is to make one automobile like another automobile, to make them all alike, to make them come from the factory all alike, just like one pin is like another when it comes from a pin factory.'[101] This resulted in the black only Model T which from 1907 to 1925 was refined both technically and in how it was produced, including in 1914 the invention of a moving line system for the chassis assembly, but was little changed in terms of its form. Inspite of the car's performance and, indeed, its low price – which was reduced by over half during the model's life – sales fell off in the late 1920s and Ford was forced to bring out a new model which looked different. The Model A was introduced in 1927. The critic, Werner Gräff, writing 'On the form of the motor car' in 1925-6 observed: 'We Europeans pride ourselves on the fact that we disappointed Henry Ford by not adopting his motor car as widely as he expected, in spite of its extraordinary cheapness and reliability. We are also rather pleased that as a result he has recently decided to concern himself with its form.'[102] While styling can be presented as a way of providing built-in obsolesence to the advantage of industry, this statement suggests that it is welcomed just as much by the consumer.

The power of the consumer has been recognised during this century as never before. The message of Edward A.Filene's *Successful living in this machine age*[103] was that the new machine civilisation was to

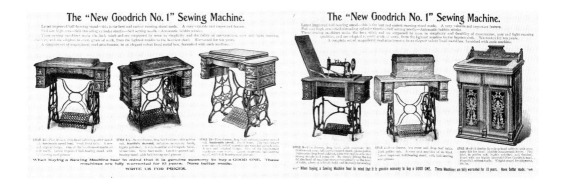

be ruled by the taste and wants of the masses, the people who represent the greatest volume of buying power. The British critic and historian, John Gloag, in a review of this book, went so far as to blame the American Depression on the earner's neglect of his duty of spending: 'He wanted to get rich quick on paper, and saved and invested instead of spending and speeding-up industry, and thereby replaced the benevolent circle by a vicious one of over-production, wage-cuts, lower purchasing power, the slowing-up of industrial output, and finally unemployment'.[104]

Indeed pleasing the consumer has even been presented as a form of functionalism which of course it is. Alfred Barr, at the time Director of the Museum of Modern Art, New York, wrote in the preface to the book published in 1932 which, with the exhibition it accompanied, coined the term the 'International Style:' 'American skyscraper architects with cynical good humour have been willing to label their capricious facade ornament "functional" – "One function of the building is to please the client" '.[105]

The consumer is frequently taken as the starting point for a new product. An example is the brief for the Psion Organiser, a hand-held computer, conceived as an electronic 'filofax', which revolved around an imaginary character called Roger. 'Roger goes to work in a suit, but he would not be seen dead in a suit among his social "set". Roger likes to be serious, efficient and organised at work, but in leisure he would like to be seen with his Sony Walkman... Here we have a big problem. How do we sell to Roger – Roger at

52. Leaflet advertising sewing machines issued by Foley & Williams MFC. Co., Cincinnati, Ohio, USA c.1910.
E.2020 – 1991

Early sewing machines, used only in the work-place, had their mechanical parts exposed. Their encasement was vital to their acceptance as furniture suitable for the home. The models advertised here had cases of 'rich golden oak, beautifully decorated'.

53-54. Two products
providing examples of
different imperatives
to form:

53. Verde 700. Chair
designed by Simo Heikkilä
(Finnish, b.1943) and Yrjö
Wiherheimo (Finnish,
b.1941), 1978-9; made
by Vivero Oy, Helsinki,
Finland, 1979-80. Tubular
steel frame, metal springs,
metal and plastic fittings;
laminated birch upholstery.
Height: 124.5 cm.
W.7 – 1981

Part of the brief for the
Verde range, designed
for use in public areas
such as ships, hospitals
and auditoriums, was
that it use the skills of
redundant workers from
non-furniture industries,
and existing machinery
in existing factories. Its
form was, therefore,
driven by the skills and
equipment available.

54. Baby bath designed
by Martyn Rowlands
(British, b.1923); made by
Ekco Plastics, Southend-
on-Sea, Essex, 1957.
Polythene on wooden
base. Height: 53.3 cm.
Circ.230 – 1963

Rowlands was head of
industrial design at Ekco
plastics in the 1950s, and it
was his responsibility to
identify products which
would use the inherent
qualities of plastics to
advantage. The virtue of
this bath is that it is both
warmer and softer than a
traditional metal bath.

work or Roger, the swinger?' Two different image types for the different aspects of Roger's character were outlined and then fused to arrive at:

> 'QUALITY styling in quality high–tech shapes and
> materials but with friendly line
> PORSCHE image
> TRON style
> e.g. black (Frazer) design but with line or element of
> shocking pink or lime green
> Tron black battletank with pink cursor
> possible dark clear plastic with etched perspective
> purple or lime green perspective lines
> name: such as "Psion SEARCHER"
> (also think of Columbia space-shuttle)
> note: definitely not metallic or aluminium look
> – too common and not distinctive from calcs,
> TRON LOOK'.[106] (Fig. 35)

The power of the consumer to influence form in practice is suggested by how the clothes' manufacturer and retailer, Benetton, which has 5000 shops around the world, organises its production. Electronic liaison between factories, warehouses and shops means that what is made is dictated by what is popular at the point of sale.[107]

The twentieth century has also been the century of ergonomics, the study of the psychological and physical factors that can be used to improve the design of products for human use. This frequently affects

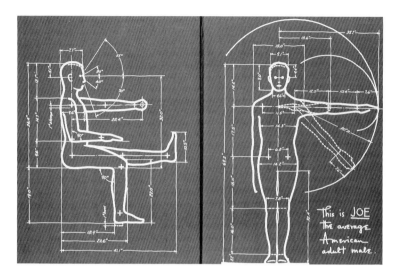

55. Fly-leaf to Henry Dreyfuss, *Designing for people*, New York 1955.

The illustration shows Joe, the average human male, who with Josephine represented for the Dreyfuss office 'the millions of consumers for whom we are designing, and they dictate every line we draw'.

their outward form. Henry Dreyfuss, in his account of his working life, published under the title *Designing for people* in 1955, claimed: 'For years in our office we have kept before us the concept that what we are working on is going to be ridden in, sat upon, looked at, talked into, activated, operated, or in some way used by people individually or en masse. If the point of contact between the product and the people becomes a point of friction, then the industrial designer has failed. If, on the other hand, people are made safer, more comfortable, more eager to purchase, more efficient – or just plain happier – the designer has succeeded'[108] (Fig. 55).

Consumers' wishes remain of the utmost importance to manufacturers even in the case of those, like Braun, which are associated with a rationalist approach to design and some notion of objective excellence. Braun's 'first Commandment for product development…is to cater to the true needs of the people for whom (the products) are intended. The products should be and look exactly as these people wish the objects with which they live to be and look.'[109] What consumers want is not, however, driven by the rationalist principles that guide the form–givers. The success of Braun lies surely as much in the discernment the selection of a Braun product implies as in the form of the chosen product, even if the consumer does not quite understand from whence the brand's prestige comes.[110]

56. Advertisement for the Maxima range, designed by Max Clendinning (British, b.1930), manufactured by Race Furniture Ltd, 1966-c.1970

Clendinning argued that 'In the 18th and 19th centuries they had chairs to fit their big skirts. Mini skirts should make a difference to chair design'. The Maxima range consisted of twenty-five standard parts which purchasers could assemble according to their requirements.

57. Car brochure, issued by Chrysler Division, Chrysler Corporation, Detroit, USA 1955.
E.2013-1991

The brochure, offering six variations on two different 1956 models, claims that the Chrysler is 'Now...more than ever America's most smartly different car'. The figures grouped beside the different models are themselves carefully differentiated also.

Form and Identity

'So what do we mean by furniture? "*The means by which we make our social rank known*" This, very precisely, is the way kings think: Louis XIV was a brilliant exponent of this mentality. Shall we be Louis XIVs?'. So wrote Le Corbusier in 1929, rejecting this image in favour of one of furniture as 'tools' and 'servants' which serve our needs.[111] In the same vein Marcel Breuer stated: 'The new living space should not be a self-portrait of the architect, nor should it immediately convey the individual personality of the occupant'.[112] But the very expression of these sentiments makes clear the role played by form in the expression of identity, a need and function of a kind but distinct from the Modernist restriction of the term to practical utility. This section looks at alternative interpretations of the notion of function (Figs. 58 and 59).

In fact a formal language symbolic of the times was exactly what the artists, architects and designers associated with functionalist theories and machine imagery were looking for be they the Russian avant-garde with their fantastical constructions or American industrialists with their streamlined stationary products. Machine imagery and forms associated with the machine were used to express faith in their power even though their power was not necessarily employed. This is shown especially clearly in the work of the British painter Edward Wadsworth (1889-1949), who trained as an engineer before becoming an artist. Although machines formed the subject matter of his work and he even portrayed them in a vocabulary derived from their constituent parts – nuts, bolts and cogs – to multiply these images, he favoured the hand-technique of woodcutting in use by the fourteenth century rather than one of the recently introduced photo-mechanical processes (Fig. 12).

Adolf Loos highlighted the symbolic nature of form in architecture in general: 'The task of the architect is…to define what the feelings (it arouses in people) should be. The room must look comfortable, the house cosy. The court-house must make a threatening impression on the furtive criminal. The bank building must say, 'Here your

58-59. Two twentieth-century chairs which suggest some of the messages delivered by form:

58. Chair designed and made by André Groult (French, 1884-1967), fabric by Paul Follot (French, 1877-1941), France, c.1920. Ebony and stained maple, upholstered in brocaded silk. Height: 103.5 cm. W.45-2981

This chair, part of a large bedroom suite made for a Paris apartment of which its designer was the interior decorator, is in a modified Louis XVI style, mediated by nineteenth-century interpretations. Furniture of a grand historicising character sets its users in a grand lineage.

59. 'Orkney'. Chair made by Reynold Eunson (British), Kirwall, Orkney, Britain, 1971. Fumed oak frame with brass screws, 'sandy oat' straw back strengthened with twine. Height: 106.7 cm. Circ.120 – 1971

This variant of the vernacular frame and straw chair has a history stretching back through centuries. Its manufacture in the second half of the twentieth century contains a statement about the value attached to rural traditions and places its buyer as someone sharing those values.

money is securely safeguarded by honest people'[113] (Figs. 60 and 61). The architect and theatre designer Hans Poelzig (1869-1936) referred to the symbolic nature of Modernist architecture in particular: 'Why after all, is the current style of building successful?' he asked. 'For practical reasons?…Is the flat roof preferred on purely practical grounds? This particular form predominates because it is the new symbol of a new way of life, which corresponds to the current hunger for light and air. The sensitive layman would sooner be palmed off with a house by some gifted artisan which is completely unpractical but has the form which he likes, than move to some perfectly practical form of housing which nevertheless seems to him without form: he seeks an enrichment of his emotional life.'[114]

Individual choices of form are equally affected by our self-image and how we wish others to perceive us. The truth of this in terms of clothing is self-evident (Figs. 62-4) but it is true also in our choice of less personal accoutrements, including machines themselves. In an article which explores the function and design of the automobile, psychologists Peter Marsh and Peter Collett argue: 'The car as primarily a form of personal transportation does not make sense. If that were all it really did for us, we would get rid of it and develop much more rational solutions…The car is principally

60 & 61. Exterior and
interior views of the Lloyds
Building, London, designed
by Richard Rogers (British,
b.1933) and built by
Bovis, 1979-84.
Lloyds of London

Iconographically the
building with its modular
construction and its
exposed services appears
to say that it, and by
extension the business
within, has no secrets. Its
council meetings, however,
are held in an eighteenth-
century room designed by
the Neo-classicist Robert
Adam (1728-1792),
removed from Bowood
House and carefully
reconstructed on the
eleventh floor. Lloyds'
business heart, thus, calls
into play a formal language
long associated with power.

a medium of expression – a way of saying who we are and where we belong in the social order of things.' They back up their thesis with the findings of a MORI survey which showed, for example, that young, trendy and aggressive drivers were associated with cars such as VW Golfs, the family-oriented middle-aged with Volvos, the professional, successful and status-conscious with Rovers and the 'warm, ordinary and friendly' with Citroen 2CVs. They also point out that these stereotypes are self-fulfilling, for when we go to buy a car we are drawn towards models which fit the image we have of ourselves[115] (Fig. 57).

Form also plays a vital part in product identity. It is through the gradual evolution of the basic lines of certain cars reinforced by the repetition of formal details such as radiator covers, badges and wheel-hubs that different models are identified as coming from the same stable. Equally formal means have been developed during the present century to provide identity for corporate businesses and multi-national companies. Manufacturers and traders have always used formal symbols to attract custom: makers' marks and shop signs are almost as old as commerce itself but as industrial techniques and communications developed in the mid-nineteenth century manufacturers began to produce distinctively packaged ranges of goods which identified their origins in a world market. The words and symbols used became combined into specific configurations giving rise to what is now called the logo. The logo has become part of a complete programme of identity in which every point of contact with the public, be it packaging, advertising, stationery, uniform or delivery vehicles, expresses through its deployment of colour and form, two- and three-dimensional, the image of the company. This image can also be expressed through the form of the actual products produced; the well-mannered pebble-like nature of many recent Braun products (Fig. 50), for example, gives them a family likeness. This is fundamental to their recognition as Braun products and, thus, to the firm's success.

Designers of other products may even call on these images to summon up the character of a new product. The designers of the Psion Organiser were told at the concept stage to 'think of the

62. Shoes designed by Vivienne Westwood (British, b.1941), 1993. Punched leather imitation snakeskin.
T.225 – 1993

These shoes were worn by 'supermodel' Naomi Campbell when she tumbled over on the catwalk modelling Vivienne Westwood's forthcoming collection in Paris. Their exceptionally high heels and thick platforms are not functional in a practical sense but they place the wearer as a member of a fashionable elite.

63. Nike Air Max running shoe, designed by Nike, California, USA, made in Korea, 1992. Plastics.
T.291 – 1992

Nike employs sixty designers and releases 500 footwear designs each year. These shoes are worn by athletes but are aimed primarily at a youthful market for which high-performance footwear is currently fashionable. They provide an example of functionalism as fashion.

64. Scroll brogues designed and made by John Lobb Co. Ltd, London, Britain, 1991. Calf leather 'navvy cut'.
T.187 – 1992

Traditional, hand-made shoes made by a firm with a Royal warrant associate their wearer, and the wearer of shoes resembling them, with 'old-world' values and a privileged way of life.

65. 'How High The Moon'. Chair designed by Shiro Kuramata (Japanese, 1934-1991), made by Vitra, Basel, Switzerland, 1986-7. Perforated steel. Height: 72 cm. W.6-1990

This self-consciously improbable piece of furniture, produced in a limited edition in the manner of sculpture, challenges our expectations thereby encouraging perception of the chair as an object to contemplate.

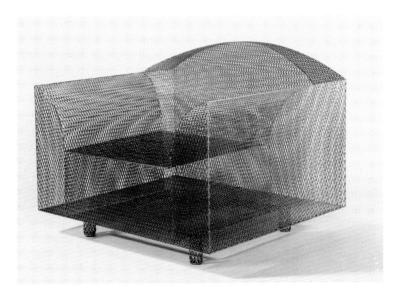

images conjured up by the words 'Porsche', 'Dunhill', 'Sony Walkman', 'Levis', 'Hewlett-Packard' or 'Harrods' and finally took 'Porsche' as their image model.[116]

Form also provides national identity. The national flag is a simple example but national characteristics can be present also in the formal language adopted across the full range of production. The streamlined skycraper imagery associated with the USA in the 1930s and the clean organic forms associated with Scandinavia in the 1950s are two instantly recognisable examples. Form is also, however, used by nations to express aims and allegiances. The adoption of Classical form with its reference to ancient power has been used for its symbolic value by many Western nations but changes in Finnish design during the century provide a more individual and specific example. Tapio Periainen, Director of the Finnish Society of Crafts and Design, wrote: 'Like architecture, design has always been of immense significance for cultural and artistic life in Finland: it expresses our national identity in a material form'. He goes on to relate the national romanticism visible in Finnish products at the turn of the century to Finland's struggle for independence and its adoption of a 'functionalist' vocabulary to its gaining of independence in 1917.[117]

Form is also its own raison d'être, even of products which many would argue belong primarily in the world of usefulness. The form of Rietveld's early armchair has already been discussed.[118] The armchair 'How High The Moon' by Shiro Kuramata (1934-1991) (Fig. 65) translates the traditional bulky and upholstered nature of the enveloping club chair into a lightweight, transparent and rigid chair in a manner which suggests that at least one of its primary functions is to examine the concept of the chair; certainly it cannot be to provide comfortable seating. Matthew Hilton's 'Antelope Table' encourages a similar analysis (Fig. 66). This sophisticated table takes as its model the three-legged table, a vernacular design associated with the cottage. A similar tension is present in the choice of MDF for the table top, a down-market material here given an exquisite surface by staining. The presentation of a static piece of furniture as if in movement further subverts our expectations. The piece does work as a table but the function of its unexpected form is also surely to ask us to consider the nature of tables, to surprise, to amuse and to set our conception of furniture free?

Both the chair and table are titled as works of art. Increasingly artists have been extending the range of their form to include

66. 'Antelope' table designed by Matthew Hilton (British, b.1957), made by SCP Ltd, London, 1987. MDF top, stainless steel insert, sycamore leg, aluminium legs. Height: 71.1 cm. W.17 – 1990

The invention of a table resembling an object capable of movement provides a new way of thinking about a static and familiar object type.

67-68. Usually typography is concerned with legibility and the efficient transmission of messages. Messages are, however, also contained within the letter's form. Two pieces of German typography printed within ten years of each other provide examples:

67. Excerpt from *Prospekt Bauhaus Dessau: Hochschule für Gestaltung* [Bauhaus Dessau: High School for Design Prospectus], design attributed to Herbert Bayer (German, 1900-1985), Dessau c.1928.

A lower-case sans serif alphabet was used by the Bauhaus. As a result it has become identified with 'progressive' design and by association with 'progressive' thought.

68. Excerpt from *Ausstellung: Malerie, Graphik, Plastik:... 1936* [Exhibition: painting, graphics, plastic art...], designed by George Goedecker, Berlin 1936.

Black letter or Gothic Script was approved as the German national type-face in 1933 since when it has been associated with Nazi propaganda.

69. *Book 91* by Keith A. Smith (USA, b.1938), Barrytown, New York 1982. L.989008859

The book structure is the vehicle of the artist's statement which in turn extends the concept of the book.

walter gropius
grundsätze der bauhaus-produktion

das bauhaus will der zeitgemäßen entwicklung der behausung dienen, vom einfachen hausgerät bis zum fertigen wohnhaus.

in der überzeugung, daß haus- und wohngerät untereinander in sinnvoller beziehung stehen müssen, sucht das bauhaus durch systematische versuchsarbeit in theorie und praxis - auf formalem, technischem und wirtschaftlichem gebiete - die gestalt jedes gegenstandes aus seinen natürlichen funktionen und bedingtheiten herauszufinden.

der moderne mensch, der sein modernes, kein historisches gewand trägt, braucht auch moderne, ihm und seiner zeit gemäße wohngehäuse mit allen der gegenwart entsprechenden dingen des täglichen gebrauches.

ein ding ist bestimmt durch sein wesen. um es so zu gestalten, daß es richtig funktioniert - ein gefäß, ein stuhl, ein haus - muß sein

Sonderschau
Siegespreise und Ehrengaben

Im Mittelraum des ersten Stockwerks und in den vier Vorderräumen des zweiten Stockwerks zeigt der Verein für deutsches Kunstgewerbe e. V. zu Berlin eine Sonderschau Siegespreise und Ehren= gaben. Die Schau enthält eine große Anzahl von Preisen und Geschenken, die im Auftrag von Behörden und Privaten bereits vergeben und freund= licherweise von den Besitzern der Ausstellung als

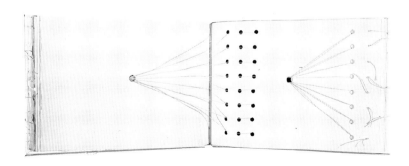

objects traditionally associated with practical functions. In a collaborative work entitled *Wild edible papers*, published in 1990, the artist and choreographer John Cage (USA, 1912–1992) turned paper, usually the passive vehicle for art, into the work itself. Edible ingredients were gathered in what the artist described as 'the physical manifestation of a conceptual pursuit' and were made into papers which not only record the 'happening' but are independent works of art in their own right.[119] Even the traditional function of the book has been subverted, its structure becoming its subject-matter. Keith A. Smith's *Book 91* is inkless and without text except for the embossed title. Its dialogue with its reader is provided by the rhythm and tensions created by the shadows cast on the pages by string and punched holes. Book becomes sculpture (Fig. 69).

Frank Lloyd Wright turned Sullivan's maxim on its head, suggesting that function derived equally from form and quoted his master as responding that his heresy was 'on a par with the old debating school argument as to which came first, the Hen or the Egg'.[120] Certainly one undeniable function of form is to provide meaning. It did this as much for the Modernists as the Post Modernists. It did it for the ancient Greeks also. These meanings may be concerned equally and simultaneously with the form's practical uses as with its potential for giving spiritual enrichment, although in any particular form and thus, product, a particular type of meaning may dominate.

70. The Stockholm Exhibition by night, 1930. Svensk Form

The easy availability of artificial light during the twentieth century has transformed the business of life in a practical sense. Light has, however, frequently been used in other ways, especially for its mood-evoking qualities. Here it outlines the flat roofs (approved Modern Movement style), drawing attention to Sweden's membership of the international avant-garde, and magnified in the water, contributes to a sense of Sweden's energy and influence.

Notes

Publications which appear in the Further Reading list at the end of this book are given by author and date only.

1 Reprinted in Louis Sullivan (1947), pp.202-213.

2 Ibid., p.203.

3 Ibid., pp.203-205.

4 Ibid., pp.207-8.

5 'What is an architect?', first published in *American Contractor*, January 1906, vol. 27, no.1, pp.48-54; quoted from Louis Sullivan (1947); p.141.

6 Auguste Choisy, *Vitruve*, Paris 1909.

7 Founder members were the architects Wells Coates and Berthold Lubetkin, and the engineer Ove Arup. Cited by Tim Benton in Paul Greenhalgh ed. (1990), p.228, n.11.

8 Bk. 1, chap. trans. Leoni, p.12, r. Quoted from E. Kaufmann (1955), pp.92-3.

9 Robert Morris, *Essay in defence of ancient architecture*, London 1728, p.18.

10 London 1793.

11 C.N.Ledoux, *L'architecture consideré sans le rapport de l'art*, Paris 1804; facsimile edition 1962, p.49.

12 Wolfgang and Anni Herrmann trans., *Marc-Antoine Laugier, an essay on architecture*, Los Angeles 1977, p.12.

13 Lodoli's views are known only through the writings of others. Francesco Conte Algarotti, 'Saggio sopra l'architettura', in *Opere*, Leghorn 1765, VI, p.209. Quoted from E. Kaufmann (1955), p.96.

14 See 13. Andreo Memmo, *Elimenti d'architettura Lodoliana, ossia l'arts del fabbricare con solidita scientifica e con eleganza non capricciosa*, Zara 1833, II, p.92. Quoted from E. Kaufmann (1955), p.243, note 171.

15 Ibid. I, p.84. Quoted from E. Kaufmann (1955) p.99.

16 C.Percier and P.F.L.Fontaine, *Recueil de décorations intérieures, comprenant tout ce qui a rapport à l'ameublement…*, Paris 1801. Trans. from 1812 edition, pp.15-16.

17 For example see Jacques-François Blondel, *Cours d'architecture*, Paris 1771-1777.

18 A.W.N.Pugin, *The true principles of pointed or christian architecture*, London 1841, p.1.

19 Ibid., p.5.

20 *Dictionnaire raisonné de l'architecture Francaise du XI au XVI siècle*, vol.IV, Paris 1854-68; Quoted from George Martin Huss, *Rational building being a translation of the article 'construction' in the Dictionnaire…*, New York 1895, pp.29-30.

21 'De la construction des édifices religieux en France depuis le commencement du christianisme jusqu'au XVIe siècle III', *Annales archéologiques*, 1845, p.325. Quoted from *Macmillan Encyclopedia of Architects*, London 1982, p.326.

22 For an exploration of this idea see J.Summerson, *Heavenly mansions*, London 1949, pp.135-158.

23 *Essai sur la peinture*, Paris 1756. Trans. from 1796 edition, p.9.

24 See page 24.

25 Edmund Burke, *A philosophical enquiry into the origin of ideas of the sublime and beautiful*, 1757; see J.T.Boulton ed., London 1958, p.105.

26 For example the briar pipe, Le Corbusier (1923); English edition Frederick Etchells trans. (1927), reprinted 1946, p.269.

27 Quoted from 1810 edition, London, p.72.

28 Horatio Greenough (1947), pp. 61-76. For analysis of Greenough's theories see Nathalia Wright (1963).

29 Louis Sullivan (1947), p.203. For related Modernist theory see p.23 below.

30 Select Committee on Arts and Manufactures, Minutes of evidence, *Parliamentary papers*, 1836, vol.IX, para. 1431; quoted from Adrian Forty (1986), p.42.

31 'The theory and organisation of the Staatliche Bauhaus', *Staatliche Bauhaus Weimar, 1919-23*, Weimar and Munich 1923, pp.7-18; quoted from Tim and Charlotte Benton with Dennis Sharp ed. (1975), p.119.

32 This theme will be further enlarged in another volume in the series: *Paradoxes of a machine age*.

33 Henry van de Velde, 'A chapter on the design and construction of modern furniture', *Pan*, vol.III, Berlin 1897, pp.260-64; quoted from Tim and Charlotte Benton with Dennis Sharp ed. (1975), p.18.

34 Henry van de Velde, 'The rôle of the engineer in modern architecture'. *Die Renaissance im modernen Kunstgewerbe*, Berlin 1901; quoted from Tim and Charlotte Benton with Dennis Sharp ed. (1975), p.33.

35 Josef Hoffmann and Koloman Moser, *Katalog mit Arbeitsprogramm der Wiener Werkstätte*, Vienna 1905; quoted from Tim and Charlotte Benton with Dennis Sharp ed. (1975), pp.36-7.

36 See Adolf Loos, *Trotzdem 1900-1931*, Innsbruck 1931, pp.81-94.

37 Paul Scheerbart, 'The functional style', chap.13, *Glasarchitektur*, Berlin 1914; quoted from Tim and Charlotte Benton with Dennis Sharp ed. (1975) p.73.

38 Quoted from Dennis Sharp in Tim and Charlotte Benton with Dennis Sharp (1975), p.xix.

39 Walter Gropius, 'The development of modern industrial architecture', *Jahrbuch des Deutschen Werkbundes*, Jena 1913, pp.17-22; quoted from Tim and Charlotte Benton with Dennis Sharp ed. (1975), p.53.

40 Hermann Muthesius, *Das englische Haus*, Berlin, 1904-5; quoted from Hermann Muthesius (1987), p.237.

41 Frank Lloyd Wright, *The art and craft of the machine*, catalogue to 14th exhibition of the Chicago Architectural Club, 1901; quoted from Frank Lloyd Wright (1992), p.62.

42 Quoted from Reyner Banham (1960) p.187.

43 Antonio Sant'Elia, 'The new city', *Nuove tendenze*, exhibition catalogue, Milan 1914; quoted from Tim and Charlotte Benton with Dennis Sharp ed. (1975), p.72.

44 'We affirm that the world's splendour has been enriched by a new beauty: the beauty of speed. A racing car whose hood is adorned with great pipes, like serpents of explosive breath – a roaring car that seems to ride on grapeshot – is more beautiful than the *Victory of Samothrace*.' Futurist manifesto, 20 February 1909. Quoted from Pontus Hulten org. (1987), p.514.

45 Walter Gropius, see note 39; quoted from Tim and Charlotte Benton with Dennis Sharp ed. (1975), p.54.

46 Fernand Léger, 'The machine aesthetic: the manufactured object, the artisan and the artist', *Bulletin de l'effort moderne*, Paris 1924; quoted from Tim and Charlotte Benton with Dennis Sharp ed. (1975), p.100.

47 Kurt Ewald, 'The beauty of machines', *Die Form*, vol.1 (new series), Berlin 1925-6, pp.117-20; quoted from Tim and Charlotte Benton with Dennis Sharp ed. (1975), p.145.

48 'Constructivisim does not imitate the machine, but it finds its equivalent in the machine's simplicity and logic.' M.Szczuka and T.Zarnower, 'What is Constructivism?', *Blok*, 6-7, Warsaw 1924; quoted from Tim and Charlotte Benton with Dennis Sharp ed. (1975), p.102.

49 Mart Stam, 'Away with the furniture artists' in Werner Gräff, *Innenraume*, Stuttgart 1928, pp.128-30; quoted from Tim and Charlotte Benton with Dennis Sharp ed. (1975), p.228.

50 Le Corbusier (1923); English edition Frederick Etchells trans. (1927), reprinted 1946, p.123.

51 This idea is explored further in another volume in the series: Jeremy Aynsley, *Nationalism and internationalism*, 1993.

52 László Moholy-Nagy, 'Constructivism and the Proletatariat', *MA*, Hungary, May 1922; quoted from Tim and Charlotte Benton with Dennis Sharp ed. (1975), p.95.

53 M.Szczuka and T.Zarnower, see note 48.

54 This idea will be explored further in another volume in the series: *Values in making*.

55 Le Corbusier (1923); English edition Frederick Etchells trans. (1927), reprinted 1946, p.126.

56 Ibid., p.127.

57 Willi Lotz, 'Suites of furniture and standard furniture design', *Die Form*, vol.II, Berlin 1927, pp.161-69; quoted from Tim and Charlotte Benton with Dennis Sharp ed. (1975), p.230.

58 Le Corbusier (1923); English edition Frederick Etchells trans. (1927), reprinted 1946, p.128.

59 Willi Lotz, see note 57.

60 Tim Benton in Paul Greenhalgh ed. (1990), p.43.

61 Le Corbusier (1923); English edition Frederick Etchells trans. (1927), reprinted 1946, p.102.

62 Ibid. p.141.

63 Ibid. p.31.

64 Royal Academy of Arts (1968), pp.22-3.

65 Published by the author, Berlin 1930, p.10; quoted from ibid., p.21.

66 Johannes Itten, 'Mein Vorkurs am Bauhaus', *Gestaltungs-und Formenlehre*, Otto Maier, Ravensburg 1963, p.81; quoted from Royal Academy of Arts (1968), p.39.

67 Reyner Banham (1960) seventh impression 1977, p.326.

68 Ibid., p.327.

69 Maurice Dufrêne, 'A survey of modern tendencies in decorative art', *The Studio yearbook of decorative art*, London 1931, pp.1-4; quoted from Tim and Charlotte Benton with Dennis Sharp ed. (1975), p.241.

70 Quoted from Bevis Hillier (1989), p. 260.

71 'Metallmöbel und moderne räumlichkeit', *Das neue Frankfurt*, vol.2, no.1, 1928, pp.11-12 trans. Royal Academy of Arts (1968) p.109; see also Christopher Wilk (1981), pp.66-67.

72 'In the cause of architecture 111: the meaning of materials – stone', *The Architectural Record*, April 1928; quoted from Frank Lloyd Wright (1992) p.270.

73 Constructivism was an international style in painting, architecture and design which deployed abstract geometric shapes in two- and three-dimensional space. It emerged from Russia in 1921. See Christina Lodder (1985).

74 See note 48.

75 Frank Granger trans., *Vitruvius on architecture*, London and New York 1931 is a convenient edition with the English beside the Latin. See especially book IV which deals with a variety of materials including bricks, lime, stone and timber.

76 See John Ruskin, 'The lamp of truth', *The Seven Lamps of Architecture*, 1849, ed., Everyman's Library, London 1969, pp.29-68.

77 For example: 'those…who are designing goods, try to get the most out of your materials, but always in such a way as honours it most. Not only should it be obvious what your material is, but something should be done with it which is specially natural to it, something which could not be done with any other.' 'Art and the beauty of the earth', a lecture by William Morris at Burslem Town Hall, 13 October 1881; quoted from H.P.Smith ed., *Documentary* 7, Oxford 1962, p.28.

78 After the closure of the Bauhaus in 1933 Josef Albers (1888-1976) emigrated to the USA, where he was an influential promoter of Bauhaus teaching methods.

79 Hannes Beckmann, *Die Gründerjahre in Bauhaus und Bauhäusler*, 1971 (note 8), p.159f; quoted from Magdalena Droste (1990), p.141-2.

80 Adolf Loos, 'Potemkin's town', *Ver Sacrum*, vol.I, Vienna 1898, pp.15-18; quoted from Tim and Charlotte Benton with Dennis Sharp ed. (1975), p.240.

81 Donald Dohner, 'Modern technique of designing', *Modern plastics*, 14 March 1937, p.71; quoted from Penny Sparke (1986) third impression 1989 p.130.

82 Quoted from Whitechapel Art Gallery, *Modern chairs 1918-1970*, London 1970, p.56.

83 Gregor Paulsson, *Vackrare vardagsvara*, Stockholm 1919, p.42; quoted from Gillian Naylor in Paul Greenhalgh ed. (1990), p.170.

84 For the history of iron and concrete construction see Sigfried Giedion (1941), pp.124-129,117-123, 129-138, 244-46, 392-406.

85 Rudolf Schindler, 'A Manifesto', Manuscript, 1912; quoted from Tim and Charlotte Benton with Dennis Sharp ed. (1975), p.113.

86 'In the cause of architecture VI: the meaning of materials – glass', *The Architectural Record*, July 1928; quoted from Frank Lloyd Wright (1992), p.291.

87 For information on plastics see Sylvia Katz (1978) and Penny Sparke (1990).

88 See Penny Sparke (1986) third impression 1989, pp.124-6.

89 See Christopher Wilk in Derek E Ostergard ed. (1987), pp.147-169 and 308-330.

90 See pages 15-16.

91 Le Corbusier, 'Mass produced buildings', *L'almanach d'architecture moderne*, Paris 1925, pp.21-23; quoted from Tim and Charlotte Benton with Dennis Sharp ed. (1975), p.134.

92 Quoted from Raymond McGrath, 'Looking into glass', *The Architectural Review Supplement – Glass*, vol.71, London 1932, p.30.

93 Quoted from Whitechapel Art Gallery, op.cit., p.58. See also Sutherland Lyall, *Hille. 75 years of British furniture*, London c.1975.

94 Quoted from Colin Naylor (1990), p.438.

95 Quoted from Norman Bel Geddes (1934), p.17.

96 Walter Gropius, 'The development of modern industrial architecture', *Jahrbuch des Deutschen Werkbundes*, Jena 1913, pp.17-22; quoted from Tim and Charlotte Benton with Dennis Sharp ed. (1975), p.53.

97 Quoted from Paul Nash, 'Going on, the artist and industry', *Week-end review*, 24 September 1932.

98 Raymond Loewy (1951) has written on the front cover in a facsimile of Loewy's hand: 'The personal record of an industrial designer from lipsticks to locomotives'.

99 Quoted from Raymond Loewy, *Industrial design*, London and Boston 1979, p.52.

100 Quoted from Henry Dreyfuss (1955), pp.14-15.

101 J.B.Rae, *The American automobile: a brief history*, Chicago 1965, p.65; quoted from Penny Sparke (1986) third impression 1989, p.9.

102 Werner Gräff, 'On the form of the motor car', *Die Form*, I (new series) Berlin 1925-6, pp.195-201; quoted from Tim and Charlotte Benton with Dennis Sharp ed. (1975), p.114.

103 New York 1931; London 1932.

104 John Gloag, 'The conquest of the machine', *The Architectural Review*, vol.72, London 1932, p.274.

105 New York, 1966 edition, p.14.

106 In the Prints, Drawings and Paintings Collection, Victoria and Albert Museum, E.2161-1991.

107 Stephen Bayley (1989), p.114.

108 Quoted from Henry Dreyfuss (1955), pp.23-4.

109 Quoted from Hugh Aldersey-Williams, *World design*, New York 1992, p.30.

110 When Dieter Rams joined Braun he worked closely with Hans Gugelot (Dutch, 1920-1965), formerly head of product design at the Hochschule für Gestaltung at Ulm, a private institution directed by Max Bill in the tradition of the Bauhaus. Rams also taught there. As a result Braun products have an aura of authority borrowed from Ulm and ultimately the Bauhaus.

111 Le Corbusier, 'The furniture adventure', *Précisions*, Vincent Fréal, Paris 1930, pp.103-122; quoted from Tim and Charlotte Benton with Dennis Sharp ed. (1975), p.234.

112 See note 71.

113 Adolf Loos, 'Architecture', written 1910 and published in various editions in German and French. Reprinted in Adolf Loos, *Trotzdem, 1990-1930*, Vienna 1931; quoted from Tim and Charlotte Benton with Dennis Sharp ed. (1975), p.45.

114 Hans Poelzig, 'The architect', *Bauwelt* 24, Berlin 1931; quoted from Tim and Charlotte Benton with Dennis Sharp ed. (1975), p.59.

115 Peter Marsh and Peter Collett, 'What's yours called', *Design Review*, Autumn, London 1992, p.48.

116 See note 106.

117 Quoted from David Revere McFadden (1982), p.255.

118 See p.25 and Fig. 20.

119 A set is in the Prints, Drawings and Paintings Collection, Victoria and Albert Museum, E.2086-1991.

120 'In the cause of architecture V: the meaning of materials – the kiln', *The architectural record*, June 1928; quoted from Frank Lloyd Wright (1992), p.288.

Further Reading

Arts Council of Great Britain, *Thirties: British art and design before the war*, exhibition catalogue, London 1979
An excellent introduction to a decade of British art and design, including a wide range of images.

Banham, Reyner *Theory and design in the first machine age*, Architectural Press, London 1960
One of the first and most important analyses of the emergence of a machine aesthetic during the first two decades of the twentieth century, embracing fine art, architecture and design.

Bayley, Stephen, *Commerce and culture from pre-industrial art to post-industrial value*, A Design Museum Book, London 1989
A mélange of recent and republished essays which present a revision of the relationship of commerce and culture.

Benton, Tim & Charlotte with Sharp, Dennis *Form follows function – a source book for the history of architecture and design 1890-1939*, The Open University Press, London 1975
An invaluable selection of extracts from the writings of designers, architects and critics of many nationalities, translated into English.

Burkhardt, Francois and Franksen, Inez ed. *Design Dieter Rams &*, Gerhardt verlag, Berlin 1980
A case study of one designer by a variety of writers suggests the interrelationship of technological, cultural and biographical aspects in design.

Collins, Michael and Papadakis, Andreas *Post-modern design*, Rizzoli, New York 1989
A lavishly illustrated study of Post-Modernism concentrating on the applied arts.

Dormer, Peter intro. *The illustrated dictionary of twentieth-century designers*, Headline, London 1991
Gives equal prominence to hand- and industrially-made products while implying a canon of design.

Droste, Magdalena *Bauhaus 1919-1933*, Benedikt Taschen, Cologne 1990
An accessible history published under the auspices of the Bauhaus-Archiv, Museum für Gestaltung. It draws on primary sources, provides useful biographies and is well illustrated.

Dreyfuss, Henry *Designing for people*, Simon and Schuster, New York 1955
A lively account of all aspects of an industrial design business by one of the first generation of American industrial designers.

Forty, Adrian *Objects of desire – design and society 1750-1980*, Thames and Hudson, London 1986
A stimulating study of the reasons underlying the appearance of man-made goods.

Geddes, Norman Bel *Horizons in industrial design*, John Lane, The Bodley Head, London 1934
An account of industrial design practice, placing it in the tradition of the fine arts, by the designer most closely associated with streamlining.

Giedion, Sigfried *Space, time and architecture, the growth of a new tradition*, Harvard University Press, Cambridge, Mass. 1941
A wide-ranging study which relates changes in architecture to the achievements of industry and the changing requirements of the population.

Greenhalgh, Paul ed. *Modernism in Design*, Reaktion Books, London 1990
Ten recent essays addressing the tenets of Modernism. Especially relevant are Tim Benton's 'The myth of function', a reappraisal of the role of function in Modernism, pp.41-52 and Gillian Naylor's 'Swedish Grace…or the acceptable face of Modernism?', pp.164-183, a case-study of national and international ingredients of Modernism.

Hillier, Bevis *Young Betjeman*, John Murray, London 1988; paperback Cardinal by Sphere Books, London 1989
A lively biography which suggests the part played by the taste of strategically placed individuals in the establishment of movements in design.

Horatio Greenough, *Form and function remarks on art by Horatio Greenough* edited by H.A.Small, University of California Press, Berkley and Los Angeles 1947
Provides a first-hand and readable insight into architectural thought in the nineteenth century.

Hulten, Pontus *Futurism & futurisms*, Thames and Hudson, London 1987
First published to accompany the exhibition 'Futurismo & futurismi' held at Palazzo Grassi, Venice, 1986. Profusely illustrated and organised like an encyclopedia, it provides considerable detailed information in a manner which helps you find what you want.

Jackson, Lesley *The new look: design in the fifties,* Thames and Hudson, London 1991
Published to accompany the exhibition of the same title organised by Manchester City Art Galleries. It provides a useful look at the design of a particular decade and through its illustrations provides an example of how certain forms and decorative motifs predominate at certain periods.

Jaffé, Hans Ludwig *De Stijl, 1917-1931: the Dutch contribution to modern art*, Belknap Press of Harvard University Press, Cambridge, Mass. 1986
A comprehensive study of the sources and significance of De Stijl.

Jencks, Charles *The language of Post-modern architecture*, Rizzoli, New York 1977
A study of architecture viewed as a reaction against Modernism by the person who coined the term Post-modernism.

Katz, Sylvia *Plastics designs and materials*, Studio Vista, London 1978
A clear account of the chemistry and uses of plastics with a useful glossary of terms.

Kaufmann, Emil *Architecture in the Age of Reason*, Harvard University Press, Cambridge, 1955
An excellent account of the architectural theory inherited by the twentieth century.

Lambert, Susan and Murdoch, John 'From to-day 'Modernism' is dead! Functionalism as style?' *The V&A album 5*, De Montford Publishing, London 1986, pp.206-216
An article on the changing appearance of so-called functional design.

Le Corbusier, *Vers une architecture*, Éditions Crès, Paris 1923; translated by Etchells, F. *Towards a new architecture*, Architectural Press, London 1927; later edition 1946
A key text on attitudes to form by one of the most influential architects of the century.

Lodder, Christina *Russian constructivism*, Yale University Press, New Haven and London 1985
Excellent, well-illustrated account with extensive bibliography.

Loewy, Raymond *Never leave well enough alone*, Simon and Schuster, New York 1951
The autobiography of one of the century's first and most flamboyant industrial designers.

McFadden, David Revere ed. *Scandinavian modern design, 1880-1980*, Abrams, New York 1982
Essays by a variety of authors on aspects of Scandinavian design written to accompany an exhibition at the Cooper Hewitt Museum.

Naylor, Colin ed. *Contemporary designers*, St James Press, Chicago and London 1990
A useful dictionary in which biographies and critical analyses are juxtaposed with designers' statements.

Ostergard, Derek E. ed. *Bentwood and metal furniture 1850-1946*, University of Washington Press, American Federation of Arts, New York 1987
An excellent study in which Christopher Wilk's contributions on Aalto, Breuer, Eames and Le Corbusier are especially perspicacious.

Overy, Paul *De Stijl*, Thames and Hudson, London 1991
An interesting, accessible and sound introduction to this movement.

Pevsner, Nikolaus *Pioneers of modern design*, first published under the title *Pioneers of the Modern Movement* by Faber and Faber, London 1936; latest edition Penguin Books Harmondsworth 1988.
A highly influential text which presents design as a progress.

Read, Herbert E. *Art and Industry. The principles of industrial design*, Faber and Faber, London 1934; fifth edition 1966
A seminal work mapping the territory of industrial design and its interaction with art.

Royal Academy of Arts, *50 years Bauhaus*, exhibition catalogue, London 1968
An excellent source of information, quotations and images assembled by among others Herbert Bayer.

Rudoe, Judy *Decorative arts 1850-1950*, British Museum Press, London 1991
An in-depth catalogue object by object of the collection of western decorative arts at the British Museum, it is a fine example of a particular type of object study.

Sparke, Penny. *An introduction to design and culture in the twentieth century*, Unwin Hyman, London, 1986
An illuminating account of the interdependence of design and culture addressed through themes.

Sparke, Penny ed. *The plastics age: from modernity to post-modernity*, Victoria & Albert Museum, London 1990
Containing essays by makers as well as consumers, this book provides a revealing account of the path of plastics.

Sullivan, Louis H. *Kindergarten chats (revised 1918) and other writings*, Wittenborn, Schultz, Inc., New York 1947
Sullivan's writings, published in the series *The Documents of Modern Art*, directed by Robert Motherwell, give a different flavour from the much quoted excerpts when read as a whole.

Wilk, Christopher *Marcel Breuer: furniture and interiors*, Architectural Press, London 1981
Originally published to accompany an exhibition at the Museum of Modern Art, New York, it provides an authoritative account of Breuer's life and theories, including many illustrations showing his furniture in context.

Woodham, Jonathan M. *Twentieth-century ornament*, Studio Vista, London 1990
An intriguing account of the relationship between ornament and meaning in the twentieth century, lavishly illustrated.

Wright, Frank Lloyd *Frank Lloyd Wright collected writings volume 1 1894-1930*, edited by B.B.Pfeiffer, Rizzoli, New York 1992
Frank Lloyd Wright was a prolific and lucid writer. This selection includes articles on the role of the machine and of process in design, and on the achievement of Wright's master, Louis Sullivan.

Wright, Nathalia *Horatio Greenough, the first American sculptor*, University of Pennsylvania Press, Philadelphia 1963
Sets nineteenth-century attitudes on function in the context of earlier theory.

Index